ALIENS

short stories on beings that don't belong

Editors:
Kitty Fitzgerald
Carol Clewlow

IRON PRESS

First published 2021 by IRON Press
5 Marden Terrace
Cullercoats
North Shields
NE30 4PD
tel +44(0)191 2531901
ironpress@xlnmail.com
www.ironpress.co.uk
Find us on Facebook

ISBN 978-1-9997636-8-8
Printed by Imprint Digital

Cover and book design, Brian Grogan and Peter Mortimer

Typeset in Georgia 9pt

IRON Press books are distributed by
NBN International
and represented by Inpress Ltd
Milburn House, Dean Street
Newcastle upon Tyne NE1 1LF
tel: +44(0)191 2308104
www.inpressbooks.co.uk

Supported using public funding by
ARTS COUNCIL ENGLAND
LOTTERY FUNDED

Aliens

The Thirteen Stories

Introduction (1) Kitty Fitzgerald

I'VE BEEN A SCIENCE FICTION – AND CONSEQUENTLY 'ALIENS' FAN – SINCE THE 1950'S WHEN, as a teenager, I used to borrow my dad's *Argosy Magazine*. Consequently I was delighted when asked to be involved with the Aliens book for IRON Press. And although the concept of aliens and science fiction has changed since then, the process did take me back to those amazing childhood experiences. Especially late night discussions with my dad on the whole concept of 'aliens' and where we – Irish immigrants – fitted into the picture: he had been picked up by Churchill's post war commissioners, playing a piano accordion on the streets of Clonmel, Co Waterford and sent to work in the collieries in Yorkshire.

Many of the stories in *Aliens* reminded me of the times discussing both Aliens and Capitalism. They covered a broad spectrum: A central character who is a tapeworm (*Robbie's Friend by Rieve Atkinson*) to a mysterious island (*The Island by Ian Inglis*) on to how to defeat traffic jams in a black hole (*Melt Water, Eileen Jones*) strange implants (*Misplaced, Sarah Tanburn*) an African who escapes to the UK only to be imprisoned (*Recoil, Pauline Plummer*) online dating (*The Dangers of Online Dating by Noreen Rees*), with writing styles as different as the subject matter and a wide range of characters. One of the shorter stories sticks specially in my mind: *Zap Zap* by Gerard Cole: An alien family arrives on Earth and there is tension as a child's seemingly harmless questions are followed by a harsh but well considered ending.

Co-editor Carol Clewlow and I read all submitted entries carefully, offering individual replies to all and in several cases we made editorial suggestion to stories we felt showed promises but still required some revision. I'm pleased to say that almost without exception, we reached peaceful agreements on these suggestions.

What a luxury it was having wonderful proof – readers, Eileen and Kate Jones, to assist with the completion of this collection. Many thanks to Carol for all her own commitment and we hope you enjoy this selection and the writers' many responses to the title *Aliens*.

Kitty Fitzgerald is probably best known for her novels, especially *Pigtopia* (Faber 2005), but she also writes stage and radio plays. IRON Press published her first story collection *Miranda's Shadow* in 2013 and in the same year she edited for IRON Press the short story anthology *Root*.

Introduction (2) Carol Clewlow

ACCORDING TO THE OXFORD ENGLISH DICTIONARY THE ADJECTIVE ALIEN COVERS A MULTITUDE of ideas. There's the one we all know, for better or worse, the outsider in a foreign country or culture. There's also 'unfamiliar and disturbing or distasteful' in the definition, and then of course there's the extra terrestrial with whom or what we are all so familiar these days. Pretty much all of these ideas pop up in the Aliens collection with many an unusual and entertaining take on the word. Those extra-terrestrials turn up in many guises. For instance, there's one defeating the traffic in a black hole with poetry. Another offers pause for thought for anyone considering online dating. Perhaps most important of all, there's a timely reminder for all of us in many of the stories of just how easy it can be, one way or another, to find ourselves the alien.

Carol Clewlow has published five novels including the best selling, *A Woman's Guide to Adultery* and the critically acclaimed *Keeping the Faith*. A former Royal Literary Fellow, she has taught creative writing at a number of universities and is a founder member of Operating Theatre (www.operatingtheatre.org.uk) for whom she writes drama on health and clinical issues.

Breakfast at Green Lawns

Fiona Ritchie Walker

'Drive – just drive!'

Rosan throws the scrap of paper with the directions towards Matias and jumps in the truck. Normally, with the front seat belt not working, she would sit in the back, but today she's not caring. All she wants is Matias to get started, try to find Golden before it's too late.

'I thought we were heading back to the tea fields this morning.' Matias stops at the end of the hotel drive as a truck hurtles past.

'I'll need to ring them.' Rosan scrambles in her bag for the work phone, realises her water bottle, sun hat and sunglasses are still in her room. 'It's all my fault.'

Matias doesn't reply, looks at the road ahead, checks his rear mirror. It's three years since he first picked up Rosan at the city airport and they've travelled together on each of her trips. He has learned when it's best to say nothing.

'OK. So I've stalled the interviews until one, told them not to bother with lunch.' Rosan throws the phone back in her bag. 'How long?'

'Maybe twenty minutes.'

'And the manager was sure he wasn't in his room?'

'Empty.'

Rosan runs her fingers through her hair, doesn't care what it looks like. Scrubs her face with her hands. 'He'll probably be on foot. Maybe we can pick him up, try to explain.'

Matias sighs. 'It will be hard for him, very hard.' He tries to smile. 'Maybe next time you should have an omelette.'

Shit, shit, shit. She says this under her breath, knows that Matias is generous enough to make no comment. What the hell was she thinking about? She's not back home. And would it have mattered that much if she'd just eaten the warm bread anyway?

'That is not toast.' Her first morning at Green Lawns. Four days ago.

'It has come from the toaster, madame, so I must believe that it is.' Tall chef with a big smile and an even bigger white hat on his head. He was wearing a name badge, 'Golden'. And underneath it, in smaller lettering, 'Breakfast Chef'. He was standing behind the hot plate with a bowl of eggs beside him and some bacon spitting on a silver dish. Rosan was at the guest side of the counter, a plate with a piece of steaming white bread on it in her hand.

'Not where I come from.' She smiled back at him and placed the bread at the top of the toaster, watched it start its rickety journey between the pale pink wires before being spat out the bottom again.

'Please.' Golden's hand gestured towards a sign. *Each slice, one toasting only. Setting must never be changed, in case of fire.*

'But that's crazy. I mean, it's on one and the maximum is ten, so the bread is never even going to change colour.' Rosan watched the slice reappear, still as pale as when it went in. 'Oh, well.' Took it back to her table where she ploughed a track through the centre of the warm bread with the fridge-cold butter, daubed Marmite from the tiny pot she always carried and pulled off a piece to eat.

'But nothing was burned or damaged,' Rosan tells Matias as she checks her watch.

'I think you will find it is the principle. Rules were broken.'

Green Lawns. Sometimes Rosan wonders where Teri in admin gets these places from. Oh, there have been some lovely hotels and guest houses, but most times someone in a bigger party, from a bigger charity, has booked out the best accommodation in the area.

On paper, the hotel sounded promising – top location for eating and sleeping for fifty miles. But driving up here, seeing so few houses or shops, so many tea fields, made Rosan lower her expectations. That first evening, when she requested her staple dish of egg and chips from the very limited menu, the waitress told her that because of her late arrival – 6.30 – the chef had already left. Yes, other staff did know how to prepare it, but the potatoes and eggs were in the storeroom, and the chef had gone to visit his brother, taking the key with him.

So after an evening of warm Coke and a banana, Rosan had been looking forward to her toast and Marmite in the morning. She'd not slept well, her room overlooking a pen which was the collection point for the abattoir, and from 4am the sound of distressed goats and sheep grew steadily louder as farmers herded them in.

'Surely you have made toast by now,' Golden had said as she fed her slice of bread back into the machine.

'I'm into double figures,' she'd laughed. 'Think that will be a record?'

'We should be at his village in five minutes,' Matias tells her.

'He was only trying to help.' Rosan feels tears prick her eyes, turns to look out of the window. They drink their soft drinks warm, their tea mixed with milk and always with sugar, she thinks. They kill chickens when I visit, present me with live ones when I'm leaving. They spend their last money on imported biscuits because they think that is what they should be serving. I come here and no matter how long I stay, I need to remember I don't belong here.

She had got up extra early this morning, taken her place by the toaster, started feeding the bread through as usual. Golden was at the hot plate, making a tomato omelette for another guest. They exchanged smiles.

'Madame, a call.' She'd put down her plate, run to reception, listened, and made signs to the man at the desk who brought her a piece of paper, a stubby pencil. So much to take down. Then suddenly she couldn't hear the voice at the other end of the line.

Rosan looks over at Matias. She's often wondered where he stays after he's dropped her off at whatever hotel or guest house she's using. Every morning he's waiting for her, bright and early, insisting that he's eaten.

She keeps counting out the overnight allowance and asking if the place he's using is clean, has running water. Yes, it is fine, he insists. But some mornings she wonders if he's slept in the truck,PAGE3 kept the money for his wife and daughter.

She thinks how eager people are to please her. Not that the charity will stop funding the projects based on anything she reports back. That's not her job; others will come and carry out evaluations. Rosan is the one asking all the personal questions, because that's what their supporters like – knowing that because they've set up a standing order, or made a one-off donation, this little girl is going to school, her sister is the first in the family to go to university, their home has electricity.

I don't know when to switch off from work, Rosan thinks, remembering the questions she asked Golden as she waited by the toaster.

Golden, the oldest son. Father dead, mother sick. Two brothers, one still at school. The first one to get a job out of his village, not to be farming. The little boy who liked to carry sticks home after school, fetch water for his mother, help with the cooking. He always told her he would be a chef one day.

Golden, the teenager who got turned down, offered to work in the kitchen for free at weekends and kept on applying. Who had been given his white uniform, tall hat, six months before and used his wages to pay for solar panels. Golden, the wage earner who wants his youngest brother to study, become a doctor.

Matias drives onto a dirt track, turns the steering wheel left, right, as they zigzag between trees and bushes. He turns off the engine when they come to a clearing with a circle of houses.

A man approaches. Golden! But no, this is his brother. Matias gets out, starts speaking. The brother goes into the house and returns with a folded white uniform, tries to give it to Rosan who is out of the truck now. She asks, 'What's going on?'

'He was dismissed on the spot, immediately after the fire alarm and the evacuation,' Matias tells her.

'But it was my fault. He was doing it for me.'

'He was breaking hotel regulations. The whole place could have burst into flames.'

'It was just a smoke alarm. The toast was burning – it happens all the time at home. We just open a window. It's no big deal.'

More talking between the two men and then translation. 'The manager saw him. Golden knew the rules. One toasting only. He knew the consequences.'

'Maybe if I speak to him.' But Golden is gone. 'What do you mean gone?'

More words she doesn't understand. Rosan is desperate for meaning.

'His brother says he has brought disgrace not only on his house, but the whole community.'

'Where is he? I can pay. I can get him his job back, write a reference.'

Matias shakes his head. 'It is, I think, like the roasted clay. I know you found it most amusing but here, it is different.'

Rosan puts her hands over her face. How could she? The photograph of the packet added to her timeline with her oh-so-clever caption. *Anyone up for roasted clay? Just bought a packet to bring home. Recommend booking a trip to the dentist if you want to try some.*

Matias' friend request and she'd clicked 'yes'. It was ages after she'd shared the photo, but the image was still there, waiting to be found. She pictures him in an internet cafe in the city, scrolling through.

My driver was so surprised to hear that I'd tried eating it, told me his wife enjoys roasted clay, but it's a little too sweet for him.

My driver. But he's so much more. Co-worker, colleague, safe hands. He has never complained when she's asked him to translate, although it's not part of the contract.

'So where's he gone?'

Matias and Golden's brother exchange words, point beyond the trees. To the river. Rosan looks at their faces. Why? There's no reply.

She takes off. Feels something snag on the sleeve of her blouse, the sound of ripping. Her feet slip on raised roots, an insect buzzes so close to her nose she can feel the vibration.

'Golden!' A startled cow backs away. Two goats begin running. She can hear the men calling her, their voices faint, can hear cracks from branches breaking. She must get to the river, pictures Golden sitting on a rock, throwing leaves into the flow. She wants to tell him, this is all my fault, I can speak to your manager, my director will write a letter. I can make this better.

Suddenly there are rocks and overhanging branches in front of her, fast, muddy water. Rosan stops, gasps in air, looks across at the other bank, too far for anyone to have swum across, reached the shore.

'Golden!'

What has she done? She has to find him, begins climbing, slipping over the river stones until she reaches a stretch of mud, sees deep footsteps, already filling up with water.

And though she's been warned about crocodiles, Rosan's shoes are off and she's wading in, cotton jeans darkening. She catches her breath, scans the water, is going in deeper when stomach spasms take over. There is only coffee to bring up, which is caught in the current and disappears from sight.

The Dangers of Online Dating

Noreen Rees

'Hi Dad.'

Why did my dad look surprised as I walked into his kitchen? And why was he hastily tucking his phone away, looking like a puppy that had its head in the fridge?

'How are things?'

'Fine. Fine. Coffee, Neil?'

This was odd. Usually I had to make it myself and there were never any biscuits. But here he was, holding out a tin of *Penguins*. He didn't seem eager to tell me his guilty secret though, and I guess if I were him I wouldn't have been either. Fifty-five, for God's sake, divorced for ages, should have the right to a private life. Yet later on, that moment bugged me. And over the next few weeks other things began to stack up, things that were out of character for him. The leather jacket, for instance. Dad arrived at our local pub, *The Dog and Whistle* for lunch, wearing a black leather biker jacket and a new pair of Levis. He'd had a haircut too. In a way it was all good, so why was I suspicious?

'What'll you have?' I asked.

'Oh I think Pie of the Day.' That at least was habitual.

We'd just finished our pudding when Dad fished a tablet out of the *Tesco* bag he'd been carrying.

'What do you need that for Dad? You hardly go on the internet.'

'Don't want to be left behind with all this new technology.'

'But what will you use it for?'

'Well emails of course, and googling things and...'

As he dried up I noticed the app. 'You're not thinking of—?'

'Oh no. it just came with the machine. Pre-loaded like.'

But Dad never lied easily. Hmm, dating. There were some dodgy desperate women out there. But back home my girlfriend Carrie was fairly positive.

'Your Dad *should* be moving on. He deserves another chance of happiness.'

'But internet dating? He can barely work his phone. He's a scammer magnet.'

'I'm sure he's a lot more aware than you give him credit for. Most people these days meet their partners online. Stop worrying.'

So I did for a while, because Carrie and I went on holiday to Tenerife. As we sat on the beach at El Medano, watching kite surfers swooping, I rang Dad.

He seemed a bit distant – well obviously he was distant – but it wasn't just geographically.

'What have you been up to then?' I asked cheerily.

'Just the usual.'

There seemed to be some sort of background noise.

'Is someone with you, Dad?'

'Yes, a friend has popped in.'

'It's my son,' Dad stage-whispered.

'Hello.' The woman's voice had a strange sort of sing-song quality.

'I am pleased to speak with you ... Neil.'

'And you,' I said lamely.

'Follow your dreams, Neil. Believe in yourself and don't give up.'

'Er ... right. Can you put my Dad on now?'

But the phone had gone dead. Carrie was philosophical.

'It's his life. Let him live it.'

'You're almost as bad as her – whoever she is – talking like a birthday card.'

A few days after our return my phone rang.

'I'd like you and Carrie to come and meet Irene.'

'Who's Irene, Dad?'

'You know, she's the young woman you spoke to on the phone.'

'Oh, yes.'

My heart descended to my converse trainers. While we'd been on holiday, it somehow wasn't true. Now it was.

'How young?' I asked.

'Well I think thirties, possibly forties.'

Oh God. That *was* young. So, that was my inheritance gone, probably. It had likely been extracted from Dad's bank account even then. But what else could I do but agree to meet for lunch in *The Dog and Whistle*?

When Carrie and I arrived it wasn't hard to spot Dad. It was a second (or possibly third) outing for the leather jacket. When he saw us, Dad got to his feet with all the excitement of a sixteen-year-old and introduced Irene.

She was perhaps a bit older than Dad's 'thirties to forties,' rather short, but slim with the sort of soft, dark red hair you find on sea anemones. Her eyes were the most striking feature though. It was as if there was an electric light behind them so that at times they appeared yellow, and sometimes green.

Her voice was ... well what can I say? Changeable. Sometimes soft, sometimes deeper – a bit like a lad when his voice begins to break. Irene seemed very distant too. I had no idea what she was thinking – how she viewed us. It was as if she'd been wired differently.

'Pleased to meet you, Irene,' I mumbled before introducing Carrie.

We sat down. I placed my beer carefully on a coaster. Carrie sat next to me, smiling awkwardly. I wondered whether Irene would choose Pie of the Day too.

'So ... er ... Irene, it's good to meet in person.'

Dad said nothing, just looked at Irene with puppy eyes. She looked back at him. Not unkindly, or pitying, but it was clear that all the running was being done by Dad.

'Your father is a very kind man,' Irene said. 'I'm sure you'll agree, Bryan, that we've had several happy dates. Your father makes me feel different and more special than anyone else in his life.'

Anyone else in his life? Where did that leave me?

'Yes,' said Dad, 'Movies, dinners, trips to the country. We've done it all, haven't we Irene?'

All? I really didn't like to think about that. Then his hand slid towards hers. Oh God.

So, obviously on that first meeting I didn't really warm to Irene. At times she seemed to be lost in thought. But then maybe that was her way of coping with having our family suddenly thrust upon her. I thought it best to give her the benefit of the doubt, get to know her a bit more.

'So where do you live, Irene?'

'Well I am not from round here.'

'Irene's just moved to the area from Slough – where Mars is you know.'

'Right. I guess you don't like the smell of chocolate in the air.'

Irene looked puzzled.

'I suppose you've never worked in the factory then?' Now I really was spouting inane rubbish, so I changed tack. 'What do you do as a job Irene?'

'I did not feel satisfied by work until I was satisfied by life. Now I am satisfied with life.'

That wasn't quite the answer I was looking for. Irene was slippery as an eel. Afterwards I asked Carrie what she thought.

'She would make a great politician. She's really good at avoiding answering a question.'

'What about how she looks? Her skin is so taut it looks almost translucent.'

'Definitely she's had work done.'

'How old do you think she is? Forties?'

'I'd say older, Neil. Did you see her hands?'

'Not really.'

'They look as if she's spent several summers in Andalucia. But, well she isn't unattractive. And your dad *has* been on his own for a long time.'

'I don't know about you but I felt as if I was being inspected, and found wanting,' I said.

'More like analysed.'

'Yeah. Do you think it'll last then, with Irene and Dad?'

'Who knows, but he certainly seems happy for now, loved up even.'

That really wasn't what I wanted to hear.

The next time I visited – without Carrie – Irene's things were all over the flat. Every shelf in the bathroom seemed to contain face cream, make-up and exotic-scented shower gel. I avoided the bedroom of course, but when Dad and I were alone in the kitchen I asked him if she'd moved in.

'I've been quite lonely these last few years, Son. Not your fault I know but—'

'Lonely? You've got the pub, and your 'Men in Sheds' group, and the cycling club.'

'But I don't have anyone special in my life.'

'You think that Irene is that special person?'

'Well she could be. It's early days. But no, she hasn't moved in. Well not yet, though she stays over sometimes.'

I tried to block those images from my mind, tried to conjure up more benign images of them having a meal together or watching YouTube.

A few weeks later there was an invite from Dad. Would Carrie and I like to come to supper with him and Irene? Maybe I could say we had to wait in for an *Amazon* delivery? Really, though, it was inevitable that we went. So, there we were that Friday evening, on Dad's doorstep with a bottle of *Bollinger* and a bouquet of mixed chrysanthemums. The smell of roasted beef wafted through the hall – that at least was hopeful. Dad took our coats and ushered us into the lounge. Irene was in the kitchen but shortly afterwards she appeared, and he put his arm round her. She held out her hand to me. It was icy, which seemed strange considering she'd been cooking. But then maybe she'd been washing salad.

'Hello Neil and Carrie. We are getting along fine now, aren't we?'

'Er … yes.'

Perhaps I'd not looked at her properly on our previous meeting, but I could see now that with the reddish hair softly framing her face, and her clear blue eyes, she was almost beautiful. Maybe I'd been wrong about her age. Perhaps she was even younger, in her twenties.

I had to concede that the meal was excellent. We all helped clear away, except Irene. Where had she gone? When I looked in the lounge it was empty. The room seemed very chilly, though the woodburner was stacked and burning. Condensation seemed to be dripping down the walls. Maybe the door to the kitchen had been left open when the vegetables were boiled? Carrie joined me in the hall and so did Dad, though he looked uncomfortable.

'Irene's just popped out for a bit,' he said.

I suppose I should have asked why Irene seemed to have dematerialised, as it were, but I just said, 'Bye Dad,' and gave him a brief hug.

'Thank her for a lovely meal,' Carrie said. 'I will.'

'Didn't you think that was odd?' I asked Carrie as we drove home.

'What, Irene not saying goodbye?'

'Yes. Exactly. I can't put my finger on it but there's just something.'

'I know what you mean. Maybe she's autistic or something. She seems very unemotional. Have you ever seen her laugh?'

'No, not really. I feel as if she would need a cue card held up with *laugh* on it.'

Later that night my phone rang.

'Dad?'

'It's Irene. She's still out there.'

'Out where?'

'I don't know. Places she goes to.'

'Should I come round?'

'No, it's all right Son. I'm sure she'll appear soon.'

At midnight my phone bleeped. Dad had sent an emoji of a fish and the text: "She swam back."

'She's back,' I told a sleeping Carrie before pulling the duvet over myself.

The next morning I was just coming to, when I saw Carrie scrolling through her phone.

'Anything the matter?'

'No, not really, Neil. Just, Irene's messaged me.'

'Did she say where she went last night?'

'No, nothing like that. She wants to meet me for coffee. And she's asked if we could go to a beauty counter afterwards. She wants my opinion on buying some new make-up.'

'You?'

'Exactly. With all her observational powers you'd have thought she'd have noticed I barely wear any make-up.'

'So are you going?'

'Might as well. I can unravel more of the mystery that is Irene. Shall I suggest we go on Sunday? We're not doing anything much are we?'

So, on Sunday morning I watched Carrie drive off as I looked forward to a lazy morning reading the papers. Almost three hours later, she was back.

'You must have done some serious make-up shopping,' I said. 'Did you buy anything?'

'Actually I did. Irene persuaded me into buying a very expensive red lipstick.'

'Which you'll leave at the back of your drawer and it'll never see the light of day again.'

'Probably.'

'So what did Irene buy?'

'Strangely, nothing. Oh she tried out lots. The assistant was desperate to sell her something but in the end she said that nothing was the right colour for her.'

'So why do you think she asked you along?'

'I've no idea. I don't know how your dad gets on with her but I find her hard work.'

A few days later I had to drop off a parcel I'd ordered for Dad. But as I turned the key in his front door there was a strange smell – a sort of fishy, biology lab smell. Although nothing was out of place in the flat, the windows were steamed up, as if Dad had been using an electric wallpaper stripper all night. It was strangely quiet too – no radio or TV, no music from his old CD player. Maybe Dad had gone out, but that too was odd. The only time you'd have seen him in the neighbourhood in the morning was usually well after eleven. And it was only eight thirty.

I walked slowly down the hall towards the lounge door, which was half open. I noticed Dad's leather jacket casually draped over the bannister, and the carpet felt wet, almost spongy as I walked.

'Dad?'

No answer. For some reason at that moment I wished he had a dog that could greet me at least. But I continued my slow, heavy steps down the hall as I held my breath. Then I heard a faint gurgling noise. Was it Dad? Was he choking? I rushed into the lounge, and into a scene of horror.

It was far, far worse than I could ever have imagined. Irene was sitting at the dining table wearing a jersey dress. That much was normal, but it was split in several places. And the reason it had split was that she had suddenly gained mass. She dominated the room, hugely emphasised by her reflection in the black glass table. And she seemed to be increasing in size as I watched. She looked in my direction – expressionless eyes, not blue or yellow but jet black. I couldn't help but notice her dress was pushed up to her waist. And she wasn't wearing underwear. But as she moved to sit on the table, what I thought I'd see wasn't there. Below her waist there was just something that looked like a wide slash, almost like a mouth. And surely that wasn't teeth, sharp incisor-like teeth? I realised the danger then, began to back away, for Irene's body had become opaque, and the reason for her increased growth was that there was a shadowy something inside her.

'Dad! Dad!' I yelled but there was only an eerie silence.

I ran into the kitchen and frantically grabbed a knife from the block. Irene – or whatever had been Irene – was now spreading out along the black glass table top, leaving a slithering trail. I pushed the knife into Irene's stomach. A gurgling hot mixture of what looked and smelled like fish guts spilled out, and there was the sound of groaning. I pulled the knife downwards, making the slit longer but as I did so, Irene began to change. Her body began to shake, and she thrashed around like a cornered sea snake. I pulled at the tear in her skin, worked the knife on it. Finally, Irene gave out a loud moan and lifted her legs. Then she shrank down like the Wicked Witch of the East until all that was left on the table was a sort of ... embryo?

My first instinct was to pick it up. The organism was small as a kidney, slimy yet strangely warm. But as I held it, it began to increase in size, adhere to my arm. Then it began sending out a sticky white substance that soon enveloped my limbs. it tightened its grip until I couldn't move, and couldn't breathe. I was panicking. The substance weaving across my lips tasted bitter and rank, like stale beer left in a dark cellar. With a huge effort, I managed to extract my phone from my jeans pocket, and ring Emergency Services.

'Ambulance!' I yelled. 'Send an ambulance quick!'

'What is the problem?'

'It's ... well ... er, I think an alien just ate my dad.'

As I said the words I knew how ridiculous it sounded, but really it seemed to be the only logical explanation.

Just at that moment, I heard a car horn. It was Carrie. Oh, Carrie! I managed to struggle along the hallway in my evil-smelling cocoon. As I reached the drive, Carrie opened the car door.

'Get in, Neil. Hurry!' she shouted.

That's when I noticed Irene at the bay window. She'd re-formed and her eyes were swivelling left and right. Her face was pale, hair framing it like the Medusa. I tried to tell Carrie but all that came out was a faint grunting. Carrie didn't seem to be shocked or afraid, though. She leaned over and dragged me into the car.

'You OK?' she asked.

'Dad—'

'I'm so sorry, Neil. There was nothing you could have done. Let's go home.'

I looked at her properly then. She was wearing bright red lipstick, and she'd done something to her hair. It was snaking around her face in tendrils.

'Carrie—'

'We're going home, Neil,' she said. 'It will be fine. You are braver than you believe.'

Then she pushed her foot down hard on the accelerator, and we roared up the road.

Don't Think Too Hard

Andrew Sutherland

So here I am, standing in the dirt with my Dutch hoe in my hands, shaking like a leaf and thinking about how long it's been going on, so long in fact that I'd almost got immune to it, but not immune enough since it's just got a whole lot worse and I can't get away from it, her living next door and all and wanting to talk to me every time I see her, which might be only twice a week or so but that's twice a week too often in anybody's book, honest to God, every time I'm out in the garden she'll stick her head over the fence and say *hello, Andrew, how are you today* and I'll say *I'm fine thanks, Denise, how are you* and then it'll start, guaranteed and for certain, off she'll go about how she's just had a long chat concerning plastic bags in the ocean with that nice Mr Attenborough, or maybe she'll want to tell me about the suspicious pair of cockney lads she'd seen in the *Queen Vic* last night and their *rather sotto voce, Andrew* conversation about a stolen van, well, the first time it happened it took me a while to cotton on that she was simply rehearsing stuff she'd seen on the telly, rehearsing it or reliving it or whatever, because as far as Denise is concerned everything on TV is real and involves her personally, she thinks *Dr Who*'s a factual investigation into the dangers of foreign travel for Christ's sake, and I've figured out she watches a lot of political chat shows as she's always banging on about having attended a protest somewhere even though I know she never leaves the house except to do her shopping and maybe go to a garden centre for potting compost on a Saturday, now don't get me wrong, I'm not mocking the woman as she clearly has issues upstairs, but it can get pretty weird because to look at her you wouldn't know that she's mad, her being one of those people who visually could be either in her late twenties or early forties or anything in between, I think they call her type of face generic, and she dresses pretty normally although relying a little too heavily on the primary colours for my taste, all of which combines to make a conversation with her quite unsettling, particularly as following her husband Malcolm's recent demise, Denise apparently signed up for *Now TV* or something, thus discovering masses of new films and made-for-TV series which I'm certain the woman binge-watches because she'll appear on her patio all wild-eyed having a complete panic attack about season six of *Game of Thrones*, and I'll have to listen to the whole thing being retold as if it was actually happening to her, right here and right now, which it clearly isn't but I'm far too polite to say so, at least back in the late '90s when all this started it used to be mostly routine government stuff she got confused about – in fact the first thing she ever said to me was *Andrew, I don't want to make a fuss but we've got twenty-four hours to save the NHS* – nowadays though it's post-apocalyptic ninja zombies shooting it out with teenage cyber vampires in her en suite shower room complete with sound effects that I can hear even with the windows closed, which is obviously and undeniably a great deal worse than it was before, I mean give me strength, how on Earth Malcolm put up with it I don't know but the man managed to keep a lid on it while he was still with us, bless him, by confining her television habits to documentaries for the most part, but now he's gone and of course her viewing's spiralling completely out of control, anyway thereby hangs a tale in its own right as Malcolm's surname was Dennis so when they got married Denise went from being Denise Fairchild to Denise Dennis and overnight became convinced that her (imaginary) best friend Debbie Harry wrote the *Blondie* song of a similar name specifically about her, well that's just dotty old Denise being charming and harmless you might think, and you'd be quite right too except for when she hears it being played in public which is exactly what happened a couple of years ago at our village fete, the song came on over the tannoy and Denise began winking significantly at the local children and nodding towards the PA tent, understandably much to the kiddies' distress, after which she was asked not to attend any more fetes, I only mention this as it helps to clarify the position I'm in stood here with my hoe in my hands and unable to move I'm that scared, all right I'll admit not all her make-believe episodes have been entirely antisocial, she did once appear in her garden with a flower behind one ear and hippy-dippy bohemian bed hair, hugging herself in an alarmingly girly way and when I asked her how she was she just smiled and said *my unusual-looking gentleman friend from under the sea has come to stay,* so I said that that was nice, *he's ever so tall, and a god to certain South Americans you know* she said, then her eyes went all big and round and, leaning right over the fence, she whispered *I think I'm going to need a plumber,* which was a jolt I can tell you but I gave her the phone number of Simon who does my plumbing and she evidently rang him, as he came round to see me a bit later, *Christ* he said *she's bonkers isn't she, and did you know her house is full of seawater,* when I gave him an old-fashioned look he added *on my mother's life, I checked every inch of her pipework and it's sound as a pound, not a leak in the place but I swear it's completely full of salt water, carpets curtains the lot, smells like being on holiday,* well that little pointer plus what she'd already told me about her boyfriend clinched it, *The Shape of Water* was evidently the film of the week for Denise but how in hell she got all that seawater in there still beats me, that was as I say one of her more benign hallucinations and has nothing to do with why I'm in such a state, oh no no no, it's all because of the storm we had yesterday evening, not a rainstorm you understand as there wasn't a cloud in the sky, more of a summertime electrical storm with lots of thunder and lightning which went on well into the night then stopped as suddenly as it had started, which was as nice as ninepence by me as it meant that this morning I could get on with the weeding in peace until, you guessed it, up pops Denise at the fence and says *well, Andrew, that was an awfully dramatic storm wasn't it* and I'm thinking to myself go away Denise, I mean seriously girl, you need to get some professional help, but being a polite chap I just went with *yes, Denise, it was* and then she said *all those lightning bolts wasn't it exciting, one of them hit my lawn what do you think about that,* not much thinks I, although all I actually said was *come on Denise, it's statistically very unlikely any of them really landed in your garden* which was a schoolboy error on my part as she did the big eye thing and tipped her head indicating I should see for myself so, like I said being as how I'm so polite, I went round to hers with my hoe over my shoulder and what do you know smack bang in the middle of her lawn there's a hole, a round one about eighteen inches across with a raised rim of dirt and stones and loads more dirt sprayed outwards over the whole garden like some four-year-old's idea of an asteroid impact or whatever, here we go I thought, bending over to take a closer look and Denise bends over too so we can peer into it together, *there* she says all pleased with herself *told you so, it's ever such a deep hole, Andrew, and when I felt around in there just now it's freezing cold rather than being warm to the touch as one might reasonably expect,* which annoyed the hell out of me, I mean for crying out loud, who digs a damn great hole in their own lawn at midnight just to impress the neighbours, so I said *let's see how deep it really is shall we, Denise* and picked up a stone from the rim, held it out over the middle of the hole and dropped it, well, after a fair old while I straightened up again and here I am hanging on to my hoe like it's going to prop me up while Denise goes all told-you-so-ish and walks back indoors to turn her telly on, just walks away like everyone's got a neighbour who can turn reality inside out so why should I be so jumpy about it, and all the while for all I know that damn stone is still falling, and it's pretty obvious that Denise is ripping off the Tom Cruise remake of *War of the Worlds* where the Martians ride down in lightning bolts to take over the world, only when Denise rips something off it's way different to how you or I would do it and I hope, I mean I really, really hope that something new on the telly catches her interest because I just heard a loud clonking noise and the little stones and bits of earth around the rim of that hole in her lawn have started skittering about and falling in, and I need her to find something else to think about before whatever it is she's woken down there decides to come up and have a look around.

Enemy Alien

Paul Brownsey

On waking, even before I kiss Tom, as you are supposed to do, I am thinking: can I hide my wrong-made nature for yet another day? This is the first thing I think every morning.

Getting up and having breakfast are the easiest times of the day, for simulation isn't needed when passing the milk or settling who gets into the bathroom first to shave. There is a bad moment when a new jar of marmalade is needed from the cupboard. I stare back and forth between the *Rose's Orange* and the *ASDA Extra Special*, finding no basis within myself for choosing between them, on account of the aliens being no good at insides, so whichever I open it will not be something I have decided. I manage to take out the *Rose's Orange*. It has within it a deep amber glow that is not of this earth; "the whole earth is full of God's glory" (Isaiah). Tom is full of his love for me but I am not full of anything.

Over breakfast Tom is sensitive to what is on my mind, for love makes you sensitive to the other.

'Look,' he says. 'Don't worry about it.'

He is referring to my Employee Appraisal with Pamela Wishart this afternoon, though he doesn't know that what worries me is that she might discover that, like the glow in the marmalade, I, too, am not of this earth.

'Just dance the dance,' he says, and his smile is so lovely and upholding, as he reaches out and touches my neck, that for the moment I need not worry about what the words mean.

On the bus to work a blonde girl who's just got on says, 'Hiya,' not to me, of course, but to a plump girl who is never going to be a contender in the love stakes so is settling for a career in which she will boss people around. The blonde girl said 'Hiya' with perfect ease, never a doubt of her welcome, for she is absolutely completely a young woman who has friends; there is no chink in her at all where such a doubt could get in.

I sustain myself by thinking of Tom, solid through and through with his love for something he doesn't know is not made right. I suppose I should feel guilty for the deceit.

Of course, I don't really believe this about aliens. It's just a theory that would fit. Suppose aliens send spies to pave the way for a takeover of the earth. The spies have to look like humans but the aliens' technology is not as advanced as they would like: they can make a perfect job of the outside, absolutely undetectable, but they can't get the inside part of you right, you just don't have the fullness of feelings that earthlings have, you just have to mimic the outsides of feelings. I have no memory of coming from another planet, but they would wipe all such memories so that I couldn't give the game away if I were interrogated, e.g. by Pamela Wishart. But no, I don't actually *believe* this. I am too empty to believe anything. Except, as you are supposed to, in Tom's love for me.

The girls seem to be medical students of some kind. They are chatting about classes they have today, with such trust that the other person likes listening to them; I cannot see any signs in their faces that this trust is just pretended. I think, *Don't worry, it's just women's nature to communicate, talk, share thoughts and feelings*, but no, it is not a gender-specific thing, it is a human thing.

The fat girl is on some sort of committee arranging something; there'll be "dancing outside".

Dance the dance.

Making me gay was actually a good move on the aliens' part, because any awkwardness, not quite fitting in, etcetera, could be put down to that, and so would be less likely to arouse any suspicion. It's a pity they got my name from some quaint old, out-of-date book.

During the morning I am, of course, apprehensive about my interview with Pamela Wishart, but I look at myself from the outside, through the monitor up there on the other planet, and see my body selflessly concentrated on its work, the ideal employee. Anyone watching would think, to adapt Gilbert and Sullivan (actually just Gilbert): what an extraordinarily engaged and focused young man that engaged and focused young man must be! (Though actually I am not young.)

Sean Hastie stops by my desk.

He says, 'You didn't complete all the fields on the applicant pages so the system can't register any of them.' I feel small, about three feet high (ha ha).

'I'll do them again.' I murmur this intimately, enjoying feeling my words sliding into his consciousness, which is overflowing with riches, for he is intensely aware of himself at every moment, in every respect: his slimness, his ears (which make me want to cry because of their intricacy and beauty), his nipples, his not-to-be-imagined cock. His long black hair is pulled back very tightly and held in a ponytail by an elastic band – just an ordinary elastic band, turquoise, looped around several times. I picture him in the morning, modestly towelled in the bathroom (for it would be unfaithful to Tom to imagine him naked), staring in the mirror, one hand holding up his tautly gathered hair behind and the other efficiently twisting the elastic band around it. His black jacket has fine white stripes and is obviously an old suit jacket. He wears it with a separate pair of black trousers, but there's no sense of him not bothering, just wearing odd clothes: rather, with a black shirt and carefully chosen black and grey criss-cross tie, he is totally *achevé* (I think that is the word).

'Great,' Sean Hastie says, which is significant, for he is not my boss so it's not his job to issue approval.

'I shouldn't be so hasty,' I say, but because there is no slack in him he can't forget himself or any part of himself, ever; and because of this he does not get my pun or, indeed, any other jokes, he is so utterly, beautifully full of himself (not in the bad sense of that phrase). If only the aliens had modelled me on him.

Dance the dance.

His aftershave – I think of diamonds in angels' crowns – fills me so completely with him that I wonder whether the gay bit is the only bit of the inside of me that really works. Not that I would be unfaithful to Tom, even if Sean Hastie came on to me, which is exactly the sort of repellent thing Sean Hastie would never do.

At lunchtime I go to the pub as usual. It is Sean Hastie's turn to get them in. (Why not just "get them"? People are so accepting of phrases, without scrutinising them properly.) I never take alcohol, because drunks babble secrets. He gets my orange juice and lemonade without even asking, which means that a preference of mine is lodged inside him like a tapeworm, and for a moment I am not an alien. But I soon remember, for whereas the other guys' comments and quips and laughter are just them being who they are and so earn respect, when I try to follow suit it feels strained and put on. This awkwardness has absolutely nothing to do with me being gay, because they are all perfectly okay about that, like when Sean Hastie tells some story about a friend who picked up a girl in Dublin on a stag weekend and she kept a cross and chain round her neck when she got all her other clothes off, and I respond with a story, as you are supposed to, about a guy I picked up in George Square – which is what happens when having no inside gets too much – who did the same and actually touched this cross in bed saying, 'If I keep this on I won't get AIDS'– well, there is this mixture of laughter and thoughtfulness from the others that is just right. This gives me the courage to look in the mirror behind the bar, and I am not picked out in a pool of ghastly green light giving away my secret; no-one could tell me apart from them except for obvious variations in hair colour, height, glasses or not, etcetera, it's just four guys up on stools having a pub lunch. In the mirror it's not really me that is driven to things like the boy with the cross, I am not responsible.

Dance the dance.

But as I said I don't really believe in the aliens. There could be a totally different explanation. For instance, the Bible says that Cain, Adam and Eve's son, went off and got married. Who to, if Adam and Eve were the first humans?

There must have been another race that wasn't human but looked sufficiently like humans for Cain to marry one. This connects with that newspaper article about scientists discovering remains of a prehistoric race that were not exactly humans, but like humans: *Homo Floresiensis*. I could be a descendant of these sub-humans. They were only about three feet tall and I am six feet tall, but their genes could have been stimulated to a growth spurt by interbreeding with humans like Cain (who, by the way, was an outcast, which is significant).

As I go into my Employee Appraisal with Pamela Wishart, strings attached to hooks in my stomach are being pulled.

Her dove-grey top, beneath a black blazer, is high and straight across, for a plunging 'V' and glimpse of tit would not befit senior management. But her hair is not at all senior management hair: it stands forth in frizzes and ringlets that make you think of women on a girls' night out at Mamma Mia. We sit across from each other in easy chairs, because it would be against the rules for us to be in a position of imbalance: she the boss behind her desk, me lowly before her in my natural position of penitent.

She says, 'Employee Appraisal is not about judging and criticising, Cuthbert. it's about making sure we are all in the field we can best function in.'

Field. She knows about my failure to complete every field on the applicant pages.

Carefully, I say nothing. Her grey trousers are cut to hide the rolls of fat which strain against some of her other outfits.

She says, 'Every human being has special gifts and Employee Appraisal is about finding what they are and moving forward.'

Every human being. Letting me know she suspects I'm not one. To fortify myself for the fight to overcome her suspicion, I try to think of Tom's love for me, as you are supposed to, but I can't find it in me. What does work is thinking: *Pamela Wishart, I may look incompetent and insignificant but one word from me and when the aliens land you will be zapped into a heap of ash by their ray guns.*

Here we go. Look, everyone, how pained I am when I confess to the fields blunder. We are supposed to *own* things – to own the unit's goals and reports and plans – and watching from the monitor up there you'd think: *boy, does he own them.* I take them right into my soul, if I had one. I make my voice tremble with intensity, my forehead knots, my eyes fix on the distance as if a closer focus is physically prevented by anguish at failing to measure up to the unit's needs.

Dancing the dance.

'––function better?'

Oh, she has been talking, I missed it. I go back to my thinking-really-sincerely look and yes, it works, because she fills the silence with what her tone tells me is essentially a repeat: 'Just one thing that would enable you to function better.'

'A candle for inside a hollowed-out pumpkin lantern,' I could answer, but of course she means, function here in the workplace, for which proper insides may not be necessary.

Why did Tom call it "dancing the dance"?

I answer her like you are supposed to. Screwing up my face like an earnest person I say, 'An HRT course might be a good idea.'

'HRT is what I need!' she jokes, for everyone laughs at the unfortunate initials that refer to Human Resources (Training), and some of her frizzes bounce; a dyed colour, more yellow than blonde.

'But, yes, that's a very good idea, Cuthbert,' she says, like someone commending me for initiative. Her pudgy mouth smiles as widely as it's capable of, and her eyes resemble shining eyes.

I was going to say that, like me, Pamela Wishart gives an excellent performance, but it is suddenly borne in on me that *it is not a performance.* WYSIWYG, What You See is What You Get. This firm insistence on management goals united with a very caring manner – she is *absolutely at one with them,* as Tom is at one with his love for me. When I realise this, my fear that she has detected my alien status vanishes absolutely, and for a few minutes I almost feel a valued person; I believe it is in my grasp to become human, if I work at it, but of course then I remember I am missing the gene for an inside. *Missing the gene* – people do use that phrase, don't they? And now here am I using it. I am programmed to pick up phrases and use them, to enable me to function. But it is worth considering seriously: that I am missing a gene. It is an alternative hypothesis to the aliens. (I have not yet picked up using *alternate* for *alternative.*)

From a folder she has been reading out some of the courses.

'That one!' I say at random, like the character in *Little Britain.* I select marmalade at random, too. It turns out I have chosen Advanced Spreadsheet Management, which is an amazing coincidence, given my failure with the fields, and I wonder whether it really is a coincidence or whether strings have been pulled to make me choose it.

When my boss says, 'Great,' with real gentleness and admiration in her eyes, absolute integrity, I am all gratitude towards her. And then I am filled with awe, because for a moment I was *all* something.

'How was it?' Tom is frying fillet steaks and has opened wine: a meal to cheer me up after my taxing day.

'How was what?'

'Your Employee Appraisal.' His voice is cosseting. He is regarding the coldness in my voice just as one of my typical oddnesses.

He smiles encouragingly. 'You danced the dance?'

'What dance?'

He says, 'Well, you know, the thing you have to do.'

He says, 'You know. You have to put on a pose of honesty and sincerity and enthusiasm for the whole fucking business. And she has to, too. Wrinkling the brow to pretend she's terribly, terribly supportive ...'

'You can't know anything about Pamela Wishart.' It must be blissful to have an inside identical with your outside. To have a self to be self-absorbed in (not in the bad sense of that phrase).

'... and you pretending you're really, really personally upset having made a balls-up of the mail stats or whatever. All steps in a dance that neither of you wants to do but you have to. All totally alien to you.'

He is staring at my face which I discover to have gone wide-eyed with horror.

I gave him the benefit of every doubt, but his using that word is final confirmation: he knows.

'Those steaks need turning,' I say, as I wait for my mind to issue the expected instruction. I sneer, 'And how do you know that's how I feel? Or rather,' I add significantly, 'I *don't* feel.'

'It's how we all feel,' he says in an unhappy manner, turning the steaks.

This unhappy manner: it's distress and weariness, distress and weariness *about me*. I am soothed to see how they go all the way through him, like letters in a stick of rock. He is my rock. *I must stop thinking like this.* His last statement reveals that things are even worse than I thought.

I once looked in his wallet and saw he kept a photograph of me there, taken the day we went to Scone Palace. He called and I turned without thinking and he snapped me, framed in an archway. You can see the Palace and peacocks in the background, and quite by accident, I actually look a nice person. The smile looks utterly spontaneous, informing you the person is totally possessed by unforced delight at being with someone for whom he has total unquestioning love. Anyone looking at this photo would say, 'What a good-looking, intelligent-looking person, a person just like any other, full of promise of everything a person should be, you'd envy someone who had that person as their partner.' Little would they know that that person is rotten in soul.

Even at the time I wondered if he'd rumbled me as an alien and the photo was to lull me into a false sense of security if I looked into his wallet, to convince me he thought of me as a normal person who could be fallen in love with. Now I realise it goes deeper than that. *It's how we all feel!* He understands me *because he is just the same*, another of the aliens' botched jobs. He, too, is just dancing the dance. He cannot really love me.

Definitely time to inaugurate the process of dumping him. At least your secret is secure when you have no-one trying to discover it.

The Island

Ian Inglis

There was nobody left alive who could remember their coming, but the legends told that they had arrived from the East in small boats. Hoping for nothing more than a safe refuge, they were unprepared for the hostility that their language and their appearance provoked. They opposed all attempts to disperse them around the country, and were eventually resettled on a small, unpopulated island and left to fend for themselves. There they remained, eking out an existence as subsistence farmers and fishermen. Apart from the occasional district inspections, they were largely ignored by the authorities. During my studies I had pieced together fragments of their story, and when I told my family of my plans to go to the island they looked at me in bewilderment.

I arrived – just as they had – on a small boat, and over the next few weeks recorded my impressions of the islanders and their way of life. Although the people were often derided by outsiders for an unwillingness to move with the times, or a reluctance to embrace new opportunities, or an inability to confront unfamiliar practices, or any number of additional perceived deficiencies, the spectacular natural beauty of the island and the evident contentment of those who lived there were powerful rejoinders to external voices who argued for the need to impose discipline and change.

The climate helped. In fact, it was impossible to separate the island from its climate. Westerly winds brought plentiful rain which helped to keep the land green and fertile. The vicissitudes of the weather – which swung between hot, dry summers and cold, wet winters, and regularly included fearsome storms, particularly in the sparsely inhabited mountainous tracts of the North – were shrugged off as an irrelevance. As long as the crops grew and the livestock flourished and the fish in the seas multiplied and the people had enough to eat, there seemed to be no good reason to consider any alternatives to a way of life that satisfied their needs.

And the character of the people also helped. Practical and resilient in their own circumstances, they maintained a robust and confident independence that occasionally led to accusations of indifference. Some travellers from the mainland reported that they were shunned by the local inhabitants and that their requests for information or attempts at conversation went unanswered. Few visitors stayed long, for the simple reason that there was nowhere to stay.

Now and again, a barn or outhouse might be called into use as overnight accommodation for those stranded there when their boats were unable to make the return crossing, and when this happened, those that stayed had nothing but praise for the unaffected and spontaneous generosity of the people they encountered.

It was said that nobody born on the island had ever left and, although this could not be verified, there was no reason to disbelieve it. The population was not large – a thousand at most – and had remained at around the same density for as long as anyone could recall. Requests from the mainland to record and note such details were disregarded, as indeed were any instructions to introduce a formal system of political representation or government. What authority there was had always been vested in a small council of elders – men and women – whose advice and discussions carried no legal weight, but which filtered down throughout the island and were quietly adopted as working practices. Crime was unknown: material possessions were shared, and the idea that one person should wish to harm or steal from or disadvantage another was seen as absurd. Education was the responsibility of each family, and took as its guiding principle the importance of preparing the young so that they could continue to contribute to the successful and efficient maintenance of the community. Their language had evolved over the years into a mixture of our own and their old, unspecified tongue. Boys and girls were treated identically, and subject to the same obligations and expectations.

While there was no evidence of organised religion, there was a strong emphasis on what could best be described as a form of geographical spirituality, based around the land, the people, and the relationship between them. Marriage was seen as unnecessary and in its place was a loose hierarchy of semi-permanent partnerships that endured only as long as both partners wished them to: such arrangements might be entered into at any age from fourteen upwards. The familiar distinctions between infancy, childhood, adolescence, adulthood and old age had little meaning. Instead, roles, duties and occupations were determined by each individual's physical abilities and by the needs of the wider group. Attempts to monitor the islanders' health were confounded by the discovery that illnesses and complaints commonplace on the mainland were entirely unknown. Personal disagreements were rare, and were quickly resolved by the immediate kin or, where this was not possible, by the council of elders. Violence or any form of physical aggression was regarded as abhorrent. Sporadic outbursts of unrest and conflict that might have threatened to spill over from nearby islands were resolutely ignored.

The people's outlook was in the present, of the present, and for the present. The absence of any historical records was matched by the absence of any historical artefacts. There were few tales of previous generations, no monuments to inspirational characters, no distinctive literary or artistic traditions of any kind, few anthropological patterns that might supply clues to the people's ancient origins. There were no discernible architectural styles or archaeological formations: houses were repaired and rebuilt as and when circumstances required, and with whatever materials were to hand at the time. And yet all this had not resulted in a mean, barren culture devoid of self-knowledge, but in a vibrant and stable community.

When I look back through the pages of my diaries, I am struck by a phrase I wrote during my first visit: "this place possesses a strange, haunting equilibrium". It is a description I find hard to better, even now. I have heard it said that to perceive infinity one need only gaze into the eyes of children or out at the waves of the sea. To these two, I would add the island's boundless and unyielding landscape: contemplation of its topography led inexorably to a subtle understanding of the balance between the tininess of an insect and the vastness of the universe.

On that first visit, I found lodgings in the house of a woman whose male companion had drowned at sea. In return for whatever manual labour I was able to provide and my assistance in caring for her three young children, I slept at the back of the building in a small room whose doorway opened directly into the stables. It was an arrangement that suited us both. I ate with the family and, like the rest of the islanders, my days began with the sunrise and ended with the sunset. I encountered none of the suspicions that would surely have accompanied such an arrangement on the mainland, and was largely left to my own devices. Although my presence was questioned by a few, there seemed to be a common understanding that one man had died and that it was therefore necessary for another man to take his place. On the one or two occasions when I was asked to account for myself, my questioner would listen without interruption to my explanation, and nod in agreement, before wishing me well.

Kajsa's children were five, six and eight years old. The proximity of their ages reflected the customary practice (which I noticed in almost all the island's families) of having children as close together as possible, in order to minimise the disruption to working life that might be caused by a series of pregnancies and births spread over several years. I guessed – although I was never told – that they had been born when she was in her early twenties. She came into my bedroom for the first time during my second month on the island. She said nothing, but pulled back the blanket and lowered herself on to me. When I made to kiss her she hesitated at first but, as if realising that some demonstration of affection would be appropriate, calmly allowed me to do so. She fell asleep in my bed, her arms and legs wrapped loosely around my body. In the early morning, she made love to me again and then returned to her own room. Once established, this pattern was repeated irregularly, perhaps once or twice a week, sometimes less, and without prior announcement. Occasionally, she would ask me to adopt a certain position or touch her in particular ways, but it seemed to me that for the most part she was less interested in giving or receiving sexual pleasure than she was in satisfying some longstanding obligation. During the day, she never spoke of our night-time meetings and her behaviour to me remained as matter-of-fact and unemotional as it always had been.

When her eldest child Roth – named after his father – failed to return home one afternoon from the nearby forest where he had been felling trees, I was somewhat taken aback to see none of the urgency that would have ensued had such an incident taken place on the mainland. It was not that the islanders were indifferent to his fate; instead, their composure reflected the community's belief that no harm would or could come to the young boy. As dusk fell, the islanders quietly assembled, lit their torches, and walked systematically through the woodland until they found him beneath a clump of bushes, nursing a sprained ankle. Roth cheerfully allowed himself to be carried home where his two sisters Rona and Aud prepared an ointment to rub on to the swollen area. By the next morning, the swelling had all but disappeared and within two days, his ankle seemed as strong as ever. That night, when Kajsa came into my bed, she made no mention of her son's mishap, and the only indication of any relief she might have felt at his safe return was in the exuberance of her lovemaking which, for the first time, expressed an awareness of both our desires.

Throughout that first summer, I enjoyed the benefits of long, open days, separated by brief periods of darkness. The Festivals of Rodull and Ljos, which were celebrated on successive days, corresponded to our own Midsummer ceremonies, and were the only holidays marked on the island. On those two days, the islanders were discouraged from doing any sort of work; instead, there were feasts and dancing, music and plays, to which all were expected to contribute. Kajsa suggested that the five of us should perform a short entertainment – I could not in all honesty call it a play – which told the tale of a young girl wandering in the mountains who loses track of time and becomes lost. She encounters an unknown but kindly creature who escorts her back to her village. My role was as the creature, Kvikindi. Aud and Rona fashioned a rough costume for me of wool and animal skins, dyed in deepening shades of yellow and brown. To lead the young girl home, I devised a loping half-walk, half-dance, which brought so much amusement to those watching that I was asked to repeat it again and again. Over the next few weeks, I watched in astonishment as my bizarre gait was incorporated by the island's children into their own games. Thereafter, I became conscious of a significant increase in my popularity on the island: I was congratulated repeatedly on my strange invention, and asked to demonstrate it to those who had the misfortune to miss its original performance. When the autumn started to move towards winter and I left for the mainland, there were tears in Kajsa's eyes as we took our farewells. It was the first time she had shown any obvious signs of emotion in my presence, and I was both surprised and humbled.

When I returned to the island several months later, Kajsa, Roth, Aud and Rona were waiting on the narrow beach for my boat to appear. Kajsa held in her arms a child – my child – who had been born during my absence, and whom she had named Arvid. My son was a strong and handsome baby, with the same contented expression as his brothers and sisters. Fatherhood was something I had never contemplated, and my initial apprehension quickly gave way to great joy as I succumbed to the unique combination of pride, anxiety and devotion that I think must afflict all new parents. When we reached the house, I found that the room in which I had previously slept was now a storeroom and pantry, and that I was to sleep with Kajsa in her bedroom.

I gradually began to think of myself not as a visitor or an outsider, but as an islander. My visits became annual events, and whenever the time came for me to leave, I found myself increasingly reluctant to go. Although there was plenty to occupy me on the mainland, and my life there was for the most part pleasant and comfortable, my thoughts remained on the island – not just with Arvid and my adopted family, but with the unhurried pace of life, the lack of pretension, and the unsullied innocence that were so different to anything I had known elsewhere. When I eventually came to my decision, it seemed so obvious that I was amazed I had not reached it before: the next time I returned to the island, I would remain there. I prepared accordingly. I took my leave of those close to me. I gave away many of my possessions, which I now realised were superfluous and would benefit others far more than they ever would me. I visited some of the special places that held happy memories for me. As I did these things, I suspected that much of my life had been – I hesitate to use the word wasted – but purposeless. The island had given me a sense of direction and I was determined to follow it to the end.

The reactions of Kajsa and the children to my news contained none of the unbridled delight that my vanity might have expected. Instead, they merely evinced a quiet satisfaction, as if I had finally understood something they had already known. I remember that summer as a glorious time. The crops were unusually plentiful, the sun shone high and bright, and among the children there was an excitement and energy I had never seen before and which seemed to spring from the land itself. If there had been any traces of doubt about the correctness of my decision, they vanished completely.

Towards the close of the summer, word came from a nearby fishing village that a young woman was nearing the end of a difficult and painful pregnancy. Her immediate neighbours, none of whom had experienced childbirth themselves, had asked for help. Kajsa and two of her closest friends, Sanna and

Marit, offered to make the short trip and, rather than follow the unnecessarily circuitous inland route, they sailed directly northwards across the wide curve of the bay. The child was delivered safely and the three women set out on their return journey in the early evening. The storm was as unexpected as it was violent. As the sky darkened and the waves grew, the westerly gale flung their small boat this way and that, before hurling it against the foot of the cliffs overlooking our village. When we scrambled over the rocks and reached the site, we found the remains of the boat strewn across the small beach. Barely conscious, Marit was clinging to part of the hull. The bodies of Sanna and Kajsa were not recovered until the next morning when the tide brought them in to the shore.

News of the accident was received with a grim resignation by the islanders. Sudden deaths were not unknown. Sanna's partner had been killed the previous winter when an avalanche in the northern mountains had caught him unawares, and Kajsa had lost Roth when his boat had capsized out at sea. Now, their women had followed them – not to the fictitious afterlife described by the purveyors of orthodox religions, but into a dark and empty place that lingered only in memory. When I told the children of their mother's death, they wept, as did I. We did not sleep that night, but sat in a circle, telling tales of Kajsa as if to preserve her unique self, and reassure ourselves of her permanent presence in our lives. The following day, the bodies were burned and the ashes scattered on the fields, as was the custom. All islanders – those that had died and those that were living – thus reasserted their spiritual connection to the land, and to the essential nature of Kajsa and Sanna.

For a while, my future seemed uncertain. The pain of my loss did not diminish and while I continued to mourn Kajsa's death, I feared that without the security of her companionship, my standing as an islander might be threatened. I also wondered if Marit felt a kind of guilt that she – who had no man or children – should have survived while Kajsa, the mother of four, had not. As her strength gradually returned, Marit began to spend much of her time with us: her company was not melancholy and she took great pleasure in playing with the children, especially with Arvid. One night, I dreamed that I was with Kajsa again: we talked of things we had done and things we had not, we drifted through the house watching the children as they slept, and as we embraced and said goodbye, I felt that a portion of my life had irretrievably ended. When I awoke, Marit lay beside me, her arms around my chest, drawing me in, claiming me as her own, granting me my refuge.

Melt Water

Eileen Jones

Watching the lone kayak thread its way through the bergs, he wondered if he would be even more afraid out there, twisting the paddle in his hands, shooting away over the green water. Against his will, his eyes switched focus to his own reflection. Beneath the fur-lined hood, a single drop of sweat trickled over his wide brow and there was a faint tic in the smooth skin below his left cheekbone. He had to control his nerves. His opening remarks to the delegates had been well received and his assistant was speeding through the last of the translations, making the weird array of grunts and whistles almost musical. But the next item was the longest and most dangerous of the day and he was dreading it.

As Selem finished speaking, Conrad turned away from the window to face his bizarre audience, and straightened his caribou-skin parka.

'And now,' he said, trying to sound confident, 'a few domestic arrangements.' It took him an hour to pick his way through the intricacies of the excretion facilities for silicon-derived life forms and the pitfalls of power cell renewal for the hybrids, but at last he was on the home stretch. 'Finally, a few housekeeping points for the carbon based delegates.' It was the event facilitator's first rule of housekeeping diplomacy: address your own life variant last.

As the delegates walked, whirred or floated towards their workshops, Selem was busy with Galaxagram posts, but Conrad had time for a coffee in his office. It's going to be OK, he thought, sipping his Aldebaranian Latte. Next renewal it might not be a gigtract he'd be signing, and then maybe ... His reverie was interrupted by the tickle of his subdermal communicator.

He switched on his console and smiled at the luminous perfection of her skin, the curtain of blue-black hair, those startling sea-green eyes ...

'I think that was OK, Selem—'

'The senior delegate from Beta Montus wishes to speak to you sir.'

He slopped coffee on to the console in shock. 'Shit! No! They haven't made it after all?' The absence of the Betans was key to the serene operation of the event. He'd been congratulating himself on his luck at their no show.

'No sir. First Delegate Primus wishes to apologise to you for the extreme delay in their arrival.' Conrad was dizzy with relief. But even transpace verbal with a Betan was torture.

'Can't you deal with it?' he wheedled.

'There's an urgent matter I must attend to, Facilitator. Two of the delegates have failed to move into their breakout zone.'

'What? Oh all right.' He had to get a grip. 'But it's not the Betans' fault they're stuck in a wormhole tailback! What have they got to apologise for?'

'Betan protocol requires it.'

'Of course it does. Stupid question.' He cleared his throat. 'So – let's do this.' That was better. He sounded more like a person in charge.

A set of thin, milky features appeared in the holitor. Primus reminded Conrad of a figure in an ancient Italian painting he'd studied in the Leisure Ac art-seg: a martyred saint, gazing piously heavenwards, one elongated finger indicating the dart that had pierced his pallid thigh.

'Please accept my sincere apologies for our continuing tardiness, esteemed Facilitator Quamanik. Unpunctuality or indeed any irregularity in public behaviour ...'

Conrad experienced a beat of malicious satisfaction, as he tried to shut out the fluting voice. Foul-ups were agony for Betans.

'Good Morning, First Delegate Primus, and please don't trouble yourself. Wormhole gridlock is beyond anyone's control.' He must be careful not to mention the main reason for the current traffic chaos: the proliferation of speculative container shipments to Andromeda after a recent spike in Galexit treaties. This threat to the union was a major theme of the conference, but Betans despised something they regarded as petty squabbling. 'And, of course, if you were to decide to cancel, we can fast-stream you detailed holominutes—'

'Cancellation is not an option, Facilitator. All Betans honour their commitments to the Galactic Economic Union. However trivial ...'

As Primus piped on, Conrad fought to stop the fizz of irritation in his bloodstream from revving into a rolling boil. 'Selem,' he pleaded, when the conversation was finally over, 'I don't care what you tell him but keep that corpse-faced whinger off my back! God! Betans! Why do they come to Actual Events? It's not like they trade with other worlds. They've got all they want on Beta Monotonous. And the only thing anyone ever imports from them is gloom. Heavily sanitised, judgemental gloom. In huge quantities.'

'Real interaction with other Galactic species is required of every Betan. At least once.'

'But, why? They think all other Galactic species are stinking barbarians.'

'The Betans believe the benefits of their encounters are entirely on the side—'

'—of the stinking barbarians. Of course.'

'I need to speak to you about the other matter sir.'

There was always another matter. But never the one he wanted to speak to her about. Needing to collect his thoughts, he went over to his narrow window to watch the latest white mountain slide into the Sound. He was a connoisseur of icebergs and this one was particularly fine. Close to the water line, the waves had tunnelled into its side, scooping out a complex labyrinth of greenish glass. The kayak was gone but, weaving among the bergs, a numerous pod of bowhead whales breached and dived in the pure water and sang their improvised melodies to one another. In the eighty-five years since President Thunberg signed The Treaty of La Paz, pollution and climatic chaos had passed into history. Earth was pristine. But, of course, there was a catch ...

His communicator was vibrating again.

'All right Selem. What is it?'

'The Triphenes sir. The two delegates still in the auditorium.'

'Don't tell me Envirosupport's crashed – not on my shift!'

'They're not ill sir. It's their behaviour ...'

'Really? Are they trashing the place?'

'You'd better see for yourself, Facilitator.'

He scanned to a view of the auditorium. The Triphenes were pink and furry. And very big. Otherwise they were pretty much indescribable. But surely they were harmless – cuddly even. They certainly seemed to be on good terms with each other, judging by the intricate entanglement of their pulsating – tentacles? – limbs? Deep in his cortex a small alarm signal chimed and he felt the nervous tic begin again in his cheek. He peered more closely at the image.

'Is that how they talk to each other –?'

'No, sir.'

'They're not ... ?'

'I'm afraid they are.'

His cheek was twitching in rhythm with the Triphenes. '*Now*? in the middle of the conference hall?'

'The female's fertile phase must have been triggered by the journey through the hypervoid.'

'Can't we have a word in their – can't we get them a room?'

'Inadvisable, sir. Triphene inter-gender congress shouldn't be interrupted. The consequences could be extreme.'

'So – how long does it take?'

'At least four hours. And we can't relocate the plenary – all the other event suites are occupied.'

On screen, the Triphenes, their pink furriness braided into a massive, quivering knot, were oblivious to everything except the heated thrust and tug of their own nature. He stared at them with a touch of envy.

'We'll have to hide them with holo-images before the delegates reassemble – it'll stretch the power budget of course—'

'With respect, sir, holo-images won't solve the problem of the noise.'

'Noise? What noise? Oh. OK. I suppose after four hours—'

'You misunderstand, sir. All Triphene reproductive activity takes place without vocalisation.'

'So – where does the noise come in?' Conrad was nervously nibbling the wolverine trim of his hood.

'They're very noisy eaters, sir. Especially the females.'

He stopped chewing fur. 'You don't mean—?'

'The phenomenon isn't unknown on Earth.'

'Only for spiders and mantises! Primitive life forms! Surely you're not telling me this poor creature's going to end up as his partner's lunch? What about his glittering career in interstellar marketing?'

'It's a sacrifice the male Triphene willingly makes. Becoming nourishment for his embryonic young is the supreme fulfilment of his destiny.'

'Tell me this will be over before the Betans get here.'

'It should be, Facilitator.'

'Thank God for that at least!' There was no way of hiding anything from an ultra-sensitive Betan. The prospect of an encounter between the two life forms was horrible.

'Try to drown it out with music, Selem. Something from Earth – something classical, not too species-specific.'

He continued to stare at the Triphenes with guilty fascination, wondering if the doomed male was relishing his last few hours. Hastily, he punched the holitor's off switch. For a moment he thought the pounding in his head had become audible, then realised that Selem was streaming an old quantosalsa mashup.

Insistent, hypnotic, the beat throbbed on. He closed his eyes and imagined clasping Selem's slim, cool body in his arms as they moved together in time to the music ... The communicator in his neck was buzzing again but the sensation seemed external and remote. He forced himself to respond.

'Yes, my— Selem?'

'Arrivals update, sir. The vessel from Beta Montus is approaching the Asteroid Net.'

'So the Betans are almost here.' He heard his own words with a sense of wonder. It was as if someone else was speaking. Someone calm, distant. 'What happened to the wormhole gridlock?' the voice continued, its tone one of politely feigned interest. 'I thought they'd be stuck for hours – days even.'

'The other traffic has dispersed.'

'*Really*. How?'

'Where possible it reversed out of the wormhole. The remaining ships blew each other up or self-destructed.'

'But, why?'

'It may only be a coincidence ...'

'Yes?'

'The Betans decided to entertain the traffic queue with a chant of their culture's edifying moral pensées. Their technology makes it impossible for other ships to block their signals.'

'And the traffic dispersal occurred soon afterwards?' It was back. That familiar note of barely suppressed panic in his voice – so familiar it was almost reassuring.

'Yes, Facilitator.'

'Hang on ... *Hang on!* Lethal poetry's banned isn't it? The Epics of Mass Destruction Protocol? *Yes!*' He punched the air. 'We'll have to detain them! Call security–'

'No sanctions apply, sir. Chants of Betan pensées continue indefinitely without rhyme or inflection, and have no line or stanza breaks. They may be lethal but they don't qualify as verse.'

His own flimsy mental shield melted and buckled. Dread began to flood in through the cracks. 'No breaks,' he moaned. 'Never any breaks.'

'You still have an hour to find a solution, Facilitator.'

'An hour! What can we do in an hour?' He knew he was in serious trouble. The Triphene munching on her terrible snack would be difficult enough to conceal from the delegates; with a party of wincing Betans there to draw attention to it, he could have a riot on his hands. Worst of all, Selem's "*You* have an hour" felt like a splinter of ice in his chest. Was she trying to distance herself from his failure? He'd thought she felt some loyalty to him at least. And surely there was something more, or a promise of something ... a spark in those beautiful eyes when he looked at her? Perhaps he should have spoken to her ... but he'd been trying to keep things professional for now. The long term was what mattered wasn't it? Hadn't he always been in this for the long term?

He slumped forward in his chair, dislodging a feather from his ornamental quiver as he pressed his knuckles into his tightly shut eyes. Long term meant permatract. The slightest blemish on his record would destroy any chance of that; it would mean transfer to a menial post on some bleak, forgotten space station. Far away from here. Far away from Selem. Because that was the big snag, the downside of the GEU: humans weren't equipped to compete in the Galactic economy, and their beautifully restored planet had become a fabulously expensive resort and dormitory suburb for those who could. For Conrad Quamanik and his generation the only hope of Earth residence was winning one of the handful of jobs in the fashionable actual event industry. Having a rare ethnic origin and looking good in your traditional costume gave you an edge – but only for as long as you didn't screw up.

He picked up the stray feather and began to rotate the shaft between his finger and thumb, noticing that the blade was shaped like a kayak paddle. Out there on the Sound, you couldn't dwell on danger. You had to stay alert, had to anticipate the shifts in the wind and the ice, meet the waves head on and skim over them. And if you did capsize, you had seconds to roll upright before the freezing water stopped your heart. He knew that swift reactions wouldn't be enough to save him here. He needed a game plan. After a moment he switched on his communicator.

'Selem, Get me the head chef.'

'The alpha grade culinary techno? Of course.'

Five hours later Conrad was arranging the disposal of a surprisingly small and clean piece of pink fur. He was feeling almost pleased with himself as he stroked the velvety fragment absently. Everything was under control. The female Triphene was aboard her star cruiser, waiting to begin her lonely voyage back to Triphenium. Lonely but not forlorn – she was radiating, as far as it was possible to tell, the sublime glow of early expectant motherhood. Or, he pondered, was it merely the glazed contentment of someone who'd just had a steamy session of inter-gender congress followed by a slap-up meal?

His relief was marred by a needle of anxiety over the Betans, who had not yet disembarked from their ship. His ruse had been a simple one. The choice on the Betans' lunch menu was minimal. The equivalent of a four-minute egg versus an egg boiled for two hundred and thirty nine seconds, was how the helpful culinary techno had explained it to him. Not, she'd hastened to add, that Betans would endure proximity to an egg, let alone eat one. He didn't want further details; what mattered was the Betans had stayed on board to debate the choice, well away from the danger zone of Triphene reproduction. Obsessing over lifestyle options was the one thing that could deflect them from their selfless missions. It was rumoured that one prominent Betan had taken a year's sabbatical to choose new envirotint for his hygiene facility. Conrad knew that Primus and his crew would stay inside their ship for many more hours, the conference forgotten. It had to be the perfect solution and he forced himself to push aside any niggling doubts. Soon his own life could begin properly. He could start to choose his own time and his own words. Words for her ears only. But for the moment, all he said was: 'Yes Selem?' into his throbbing communicator.

'An urgent message, sir. From your supervisor.'

His heart dipped to his sealskin boots. He closed his eyes.

When he opened them again the conference hall had disappeared. He and Selem were alone in a small, featureless room and she was removing the last of the sensors from his brow. He blinked and shook his head, his brain adjusting to reality and memory with the usual sinking reluctance. Selem's lovely face was as inscrutable as ever.

'I'm sorry Conrad,' she said, 'I've streamed the Admission Board's comments to your quarklet—'

'Just give me the gist.'

'You did much better this time: no immediate hostilities, some solid strategic thinking and a professional attitude. Mostly.'

'Just the outcome, please.'

'Unfortunately, exposing off-world Betans to nutritional options would have provoked a response from their ambassador.'

'Oh.'

'A mildly censorious ninety hyperbyte memo. And she would have insisted on reading it aloud.'

'At the General Assembly?'

'A prime real-time Galanet stream.'

He shuddered. 'See you next time Selem,' he said miserably, pulling on his Omega Grade hygieno-tech jacket. But he knew there wouldn't be a next time.

At the exit he stopped and turned. 'Selem – please – one last look?'

Selem's perfect features showed no sign of pity, but she adjusted a sensor and handed it to him. Pressing the pad to his temple, he was instantly back in the empty conference hall – this time with his memories brutally intact. He crossed to the window and the view of Anakut Sound. The bergs had been shunted out on the ebb tide and two more kayaks had appeared – the leading craft propelled by a woman. He knew her at once. Every night in his dreams he flew over the shining water towards her, paddling frantically to catch her up, calling out to her, until in his last few seconds of sleep she turned her lovely head and let him look into her deep-green eyes. Her real eyes. She was the real woman whose chilly synthetic reflection he knew he saw in Selem. The real woman with the melt-water eyes.

'I'm sorry,' he whispered.

As Selem watched him leave, her communicator began to buzz. Conrad's supervisor liked to wind things up promptly, if not concisely.

The screen was instantly filled with a familiar, pinched image. The vibrant turquoise of the senior mentor's tunic, with its *AndromAdventures* branding did nothing to enhance her Betan pallor.

'If he confirms the other option, will he be able to change his mind?' Selem asked.

"Absolutely not. Once they commit to ultra-space training there's no way back for any of them," is how Selem would have summarised the lengthy response.

Eventually, she was able to resume checking the test facility, picking up a goose feather – a tiny piece of reality that Conrad had chosen not to keep. She held it over the trash filter, hesitating.

Misplaced

Sarah Tanburn

'Excuse me.'

Rosalind hates having to ask. She's not Lost, she has the implant. She just doesn't know which way to go.

He peers from one side as birdies do. Her heels put them eye to eye, but he still looks down and up again, assessing her pencil skirt and shingled hair. She's obviously not Lost so he will offer advice. She says the street name, not mentioning the Court, hoping he'll take her for a journalist. He gives directions in those condescending, polite tones. Second left, first on the right.

She walks away, angry with herself for even thinking the b-word. *Navigands*, she mutters, *they're navigands*. She knows he isn't watching, not interested in the likes of her. Faulty genes, don't you know, not being able to find herself.

The police moved the Court here in the hope of reducing the crowds, but protestors are already gathering. Uniformed officers are lined up, barricades are in place. People are muttering to each other, warming their hands and stamping their feet. They sound like a distant colony of terns waking up, preparing to scream and dive on their prey.

Rosalind slips in at the back door. A plump woman, *Ava* on her name-badge, welcomes her. Unnecessary spectacles hang across her chunky bosom. That twinkle, the slight tilt to her head tell everything.

Why do I keep looking for Misplaced? Rosalind asks herself. Being an endangered species is my calling card, after all.

Ava whisks Rosalind to the temporary judge's chambers, offers refreshment, has even ironed her robes. Sweet, really. Rosalind sits at the desk, notes on-screen. Collum Accip, the defendant, put up a reasonable show. He argued the women had come on to him. He'd merely been giving them directions at their request.

If they were not Lost, his barrister said, they knew he was taking them somewhere off-track. And if they had been Lost, without the direction-sensing abilities of the navigands, maybe they only got what they deserved. After all, she suggested, for the Lost, life is so hard and rape so common they should feel flattered by assault from one such as her client. His barrister is a navigand too

Accip would pick up these women and lead them outside pretending they were going to some new venue. He didn't kill. He's too clever for that. He didn't even beat them. The victim was backed into a dead-end, unsurveilled and dark. He'd hold her up against a wall and tie her hands, gag her, force her and then leave. After a while she'd work out where she was and stagger off for help. The jury barely left the box before they convicted him.

So far, so ordinary. His speciality was the drugs. Detectives found the concoction in a jar in his flat and its effects fit the testimony. A standard date-rape derivative to make them compliant, though the women kept their memories and knew what was happening. The kicker was a cryptochrome disruptor which damaged their magsense. They could see just fine, their mapchip worked, but that ability to know where to go, their directional certainty, was dulled.

Just for a little while, they were like Rosalind. Not Lost, just Misplaced.

'I wasn't a freak as a child.'

'No,' Johnjoe smiled. 'I was the freak back then.'

'My eyes just wouldn't take modifications, not even UV protection. They tried everything to get the enzyme, the cryptochrome, into my retinas. I still remember Mum tearing the surgeons off a strip.'

'And I was born with it, one of the first, just because Mum loved her fashion and took the upgrade. I heard her one time saying to Dad, *What did we do, to have two mutants for kids?*'

They laughed together. Her brother, twenty years younger than Rosalind, is the one navigand who has always loved her.

'You still have those glasses they sold as magsense substitutes?' he asked.

'A cupboard full of them. Hot, hideous things. They don't work.'

They gazed out at the sea sparkling in the distance and his children, Thurstan and Benedicte, playing on the sand.

'You know, I'll be one of the last,' Rosalind said.

'Last what?'

'Misplaced.'

People like her, she meant. People without that direction-finding magsense which makes a navigand. She's not Lost, though, because she can tolerate an implanted mapchip.

'No-one wants children with genes like mine,' Rosalind went on. 'Not when cryptochrome, the magsense, is heritable. Not even me.'

He flushed.

'It's all right,' she reassured him, waving an arm to take it all in. 'You should be happy. Whole. You love Dani.'

'You're the judge,' he said. 'Rosalind Craffach with her stellar reputation and government politicians on speed-dial.'

'It's been fascinating, watching it unfold. Remember when Thurstan was tiny? You'd both leave the room and he'd just lie on his blanket and coo. School started and everybody else was blundering about while he just settled in.'

He looked uncertain. 'Doesn't everyone feel like that?'

'No! Of course we don't. Didn't. For all of history, we've had to learn our way. Is the toilet this way or that? Was the river to our left? You all know your place, from the very beginning.' *And it shows in everything you do.* Rosalind kept that thought to herself, being very fond of her brother's family. 'Without magsense these days you don't get work. At least I was old enough to have a career already.'

'The Lost are always with us.'

'Something like that,' she said, recalling the parade of desperate people she sees in court.

Dani came onto the verandah. 'I'm going shopping,' she said. 'Anyone want to come?'

'You taking the baby?' Johnjoe asked.

'If nobody's staying here.'

'I'll keep an eye on her,' Rosalind volunteered.

In minutes they'd piled into the car and gone.

The baby watched prisms of light on her cot, content as navigand infants always seem to be. Rosalind knew herself to be the antediluvian relic, the uncomfortable reminder that humanity had managed without magsense for millennia, an object lesson for the new generations. For a moment she forgot all of it and gloried alone in the sunshine and the silence, at peace with where she was.

Accip appealed without success. Today is his sentencing. Rosalind Craffach's job.

She sits in the stuffy room remembering her family and sunny days on the beach, and reflects that there's been little criminality directly related to the new abilities. Most of the precedents relate to health and contract law, matters of employment and the like. Judges, analysts, those who think about such things, expected someone would find a way to circumvent magsense, but Accip is the first. The first they know about.

It seems Accip concocted the drug himself, but now the bastards know it's been done the copycats will be working on it. Rosalind has talked to the public health people about an information campaign but they don't understand, not really. They're all so young they can't imagine what it's like to be Misplaced, even for a short while. That's how it is, being young – unable to imagine another life.

Accip is notorious. The press is all over the case. The public are howling. Some want him released, saying the victims must have known where they were going so they consented. Others want him hanged and seem prepared to do it themselves. Even from her chambers, she can hear the shouting has started outside.

The notes are all there: sentencing options, the summarised advice from her clerks, the closing motions, the Appeal Court judgement. She's read it all enough times, so she tilts the chair back to stare at the ceiling. The dull beige stares back, a cobweb hanging among the dust in one corner, the standard-issue lampshade further dimming the low-wattage bulb, the air dry on her lips. Punitive rage clouds her mind. She practises some breathing exercises and rolls her head around. Her focus must be on the law, on the victims, on Accip. Away from herself. She still doesn't know what sentence she will give him.

Helpful Ava knocks on the door and whispers, 'It's time, Judge Craffach.'

Rosalind shrugs on her robes and starts down the long corridor to the bland room where she will pass sentence. The passage windows are open and she can hear the hoarse cries of the crowd, some shrill young woman shrieking, 'Free Collum now!'

The noise is shut off in the insulated courtroom where the clerk snaps out, 'All rise.' Feet shuffle as she climbs the steps to the Bench.

She sits. The theatre can begin.

The defence barrister, the same diminutive woman who represented Accip throughout the case, is a bonny fighter. She lost the case, lost again on appeal, but she isn't going to let him down. She makes an impassioned speech about mercy and learning and the contrition of her client.

Rosalind studies the man standing in the dock. He is brash, his head up and eyes shining as he looks around the courtroom. His legs are apart and he balances on the balls of his feet, a cockerel ready for the pits. Every muscle in his body says *bring it on*. Rosalind keeps her face still while sighing to herself. Most prisoners are Lost. However fit he is, he won't keep that attitude for long if she sends him down. He'll learn a lot about rape.

The barrister is winding herself up to a climax.

'My Lady,' she says, perhaps sensing the judge's attention has wandered a little, 'my client deserves leniency. We are entering a new world, a world where navigands are learning new skills and unprecedented abilities. We must find new ways to manage, to police, to *judge* the morals of navigand behaviour.'

Rosalind holds up a hand. 'Are you suggesting only navigands should sit in judgment on cases involving the gifted?'

The barrister has anticipated this. 'Of course not, my lady. And your track record in understanding the complexities of a new stratum in society is second to none.'

'So what are you getting at?'

'Mr Accip is here because he is both foolish and surpassingly clever.'

The accused nods.

'He created a new drug, a medicine perhaps, but was foolish enough to test it in a particular way. But he did commit these crimes against those who could be caught out by it – other navigands.'

Accip looks down at his spread feet, so Rosalind can see only the point where his hair is pulled into an elaborate topknot. Yet she senses he is smiling. Her gavel hits the block before she knows it's in her hand.

'Look at me.'

He doesn't move.

'Mr Accip, I'm speaking to you.'

He straightens up and, yes, by god, he is grinning.

'What is so amusing, Mr Accip?'

He glances at his barrister who opens her mouth to speak.

Rosalind cuts across her. 'It's my court, Ms Erith, and I can ask any questions I feel appropriate. Mr Accip is still under oath.'

Everyone is silent. The air-conditioning murmurs and the woman on the press bench taps at her screen. Her fingers squeak.

Accip looks across at his barrister and she nods. 'You must answer.'

The man is wearing prison clothes and his hands are cuffed together in front of him. He is nearly two metres tall, and strong, but his skin already has that grey dust which comes from time inside, and the maroon tracksuit is tight at the shoulders, obviously second-hand. He looks up at the Bench and his disdain flares across the court.

'We must learn to defend ourselves,' he says. His voice is quite deep and slow, not unattractive. When he first started giving evidence Rosalind imagined him on the dance floor, saying *I brought you a drink*, and thought how seductive that might be. Now, nothing he said would excite her.

'You know about those girls cos they survived. Cos they reported,' he says. 'Kept their wits about them. We should all learn from them.'

He looks away again, hiding that smirk.

Rosalind thinks about this. He has been tried and convicted of specific offences against certain women, all of whom were navigands. He was caught because they were navigands and could give evidence of what had happened. Most of all they could say where it happened, take the police to the site. And, of course, the police believed them because most of them are birdies too these days.

'So, if they weren't navigands, you wouldn't have been caught?'

He mutters something.

'Speak up.'

He squares his shoulders and looks her straight in the eye, the mischievous dislike unmistakeable.

'You never heard about the others, did you?' His lip curls. 'Your Honour.'

Rosalind looks at his barrister – expecting shock – but she just looks resigned to her client's foolishness. Even the prosecution looks unsurprised. Rosalind realises, for the first time, that everyone else in court is a navigand. She remembers she is the only Misplaced judge left. Nobody else in this room seems offended, seems to care about victims who were Lost before he found them. She finds she is pleased to be the last Misplaced judge, to be sitting on the Bench today.

She bangs her gavel again. 'This hearing is adjourned.'

The clerk's surprised voice repeats, 'All rise,' as she sweeps out.

She paces in her temporary chambers. *How did they miss this? Did no-one check on other rape reports?* Her heart aches for those Lost girls, who vanished unnoticed by the birdies.

Accip is a hero to the evolutionists and a satan to the rest. This news will hit the street like a grenade. She remembers the journo's finger squeaking, and imagines the crowd noises are already louder.

Her world is out there. Family, friends who are navigands, some Misplaced, even a few contacts amongst the Lost. Few enough people cross those boundaries now and the tech is making the Misplaced extinct. Mapchip implants these days don't rely on magsense, but they soon will and people without it will be obsolete. Lost. Before long, no one will be sitting on the fence.

She checks her wrist and sees eleven messages already, many claiming to advise her. There's a quick *love, Jx* from Johnjoe. She only reads the one from the Minister, navigand of course, saying he will support whatever judgement she reaches. She snorts.

Rosalind lusts for ancient retaliation. *An eye for an eye.* Her fingers curve to claws. She wants to see this arrogant, violent birdie grounded and blind.

The medics can't remove the magsense without taking his sight. Maybe she should simply send him down, category A in a maximum-security prison, where he will become the victim of the Lost, not their predator.

A martyr.

No, she wants him Misplaced, vulnerable as she is vulnerable, as those women were. As all his victims became.

In the courtroom, Accip is still alert, but wary now he's had an hour to reflect on his boasting. His barrister, small and assertive as a robin, is eyeing Rosalind carefully. In her robes and elevated seat Rosalind most resembles a crow. She makes a point of looking straight at them, no sideways glances.

She reminds the court that Accip admits to more attacks than those he's been tried for, but not who or where. He has found a way to dull magsense, to make a navigand Misplaced; Rosalind is careful to describe this as a risk for everyone, a further threat to stability and safety. She laments his wasted talents. There are no precedents, she says, for this particular crime. The only way known to remove someone's magsense is to blind them and the law does not allow such punishment. This speech will be studied and broadcast so she does not say *yet*, but the implied threat hangs in the air.

'There are four parts to this sentence,' she says, 'and I order that they together make one.' The robin might fight that but she will find it hard to unravel.

'Mr Accip will have a tagging chip inserted and renewed every year, for the rest of his life.' *He will not be able to hide.*

'He will be able to move freely within one mile of his registered residence. Beyond that point he must always be blindfold.'

Rosalind hears the intake of breath but she is confident. It is analogous to a driving ban, prohibiting the use of his capabilities in the only way available.

'Should future technology enable a muffling of magsense based on geography, then he can appeal for a replacement.' Her teeth show, sharp as any cat's, as she smiles at him.

'Finally, Mr Accip will take a course, leading to a recognised qualification in advanced biochemistry. He has shown he is talented and inventive. Let him learn to use those abilities in a constructive way.'

His jaw drops. Rosalind glances at his barrister who is grimacing. Far from the traditional 'woman barrister stands up for rapist' candidate she appears to be as evolutionist as he is. Navigands, birdies, are the future, they proclaim. No use of magsense is wrong if it tests its capabilities. Humanity is growing and changing by the day and we must all celebrate.

Sentence delivered and the court empty, she stalks through the corridors to those beige chambers, where she throws the robe into a corner. When she turns to go, a woman stands in the way, dressed in cleaner's overalls. Her blazing blue eyes, common among the Lost, meet Rosalind's.

'We are marching,' she announces. 'The army of the Lost is grateful to you, Judge Craffach. We want you safe.'

She whisks out of the door. The key grates in the lock.

Rosalind realises the protestors have stopped shouting. The air is thick and heavy. Silence blankets the streets outside. Birds always stop singing just before the storm.

Recoil   Pauline Plummer

They went to a Chinese restaurant after the registry office wedding. Tony was wearing the indigo shirt she'd brought him from Sierra Leone. Her hair had been thickly braided with extensions before leaving Freetown. She slid the braids back over the shoulders of her wax print suit. They clinked bottles of Chinese lager.

'To Amina, my wife,' he said, smiling. He'd gelled his light brown hair and the front section stuck up at an angle. She looked at his face between mouthfuls of prawns and rice. It looked different in the grey light of a northern English town. In Sierra Leone he'd been tanned, with a scattering of freckles, his hair streaked blonde from the sun. Now his skin was the colour of a peeled yam.

'They can't send you back from this point on,' he said. 'As long as we stay married.'

She nodded. The knot in her gut was relaxing because of the beer. May God bless us. What else could she have done but come to England and marry the English man who'd been working in her country? Wasn't that the best for her son Solomon?

It had been so painful, looking down from the ferry at the dockside below. She saw his small face and that of her mother disappearing, as the rusty ferry crossed the swirling currents of the estuary to the airport on the other side.

'I'll come and get you, Solomon,' her words lost in the shouts, arguments, laughter of people pressed together around her.

Tony lit candles in the fire grate. They sat down on the leathery sofa and he began to undress her. 'You've put on a bit of weight, haven't you?' He screwed up his pale blue eyes. 'Still curvy though. Luver...ly.' He put out his tongue and waggled it. 'You've been a good girl have you Amina? No other man since I left?'

'No-one,' she said. 'I'm not that kind of woman.'

She got used to the machines in his house, smiling when she took the washing out, damp and smelling of flowers. While Tony was on a training course at the hospital she cooked, using the spices brought with her. It smelled like home.

Would she ever get used to the chill in the air, even during daytime? She walked to the corner shop wrapped in Tony's puffa jacket. The next door neighbour was outside. Amina waved and said 'Good afternoon, Ma.' The woman looked at her and slammed the front door behind her.

After the evening meal, Tony would lie down in front of the TV and roll a joint with the ganja that Amina had smuggled, wrapped in smoked fish and plastic.

'Why did you ask me to bring that? Can't you buy it here?'

He nodded. 'Your local stuff is so much better.'

'It was risky. And it's not good for you. You forget what I've seen.' Images from the war, images she preferred to forget, flashed across her mind. Crazed rebel soldiers in vehicles screaming past, leaving a trail of ganja.

'Stop preaching. Chill.' He patted the seat next to him so she sat down, trying to make sense of the comedy show until she gave up and went to bring in washing off the line.

He shouted through to her. 'My kids want to meet you on Friday after school.' In the photos they looked sweet with their blonde hair and big smiles. Surely they would like her when they saw what a good person she was, hardworking, loving. And they would get to meet Solomon one day. They would be his step-family.

On Friday they turned up, both taller than her. The girl was so pretty with her long blonde ponytail. She was shy, but wearing her uniform with a very short skirt. The older boy wore baggy clothes and wanted her to twist his hair into dreadlocks. She started combing and twisting the strands. Tony came in smoking a spliff and passed it to his son. She looked from one to the other, frowning.

'Tony, no,' she said. He laughed and went off, muttering.

They gave a party to celebrate. Amina cooked pots of fried rice, fufu, groundnut fish stew, hot pepper chicken, plantain and salads. His friends turned up, carrying bottles. A woman with hennaed hair helped her get out all the bowls, plates and cutlery. Tony called Amina in to introduce her to his friends. 'My wife, Amina,' he said 'Gorgeous. Look at that figure.' She rubbed her hands down her skirt. Is this how men introduce their wives here?

The friends had different jobs, she found out – some working for the council or the local paper, a job centre worker, a teacher, a social worker, Labour Party members, men who worked on the rigs like Tony. They drank all the beer and wine and then danced in the small space of the sitting room. Others stood around the back door smoking and talking. A few asked questions about life back home.

Tony rushed off to Aberdeen the next morning, back to his job as a medic. It felt lonely to see his car disappearing up the street. She counted the cash Tony had left for her, the shiny plastic notes slipping out of her hands.

When he came back after a month he pressed her into him and pulled her to the sofa. As he lay back sated, she leaned on one elbow looking at him.

'I need to work, Tony. I need to make money to send home. It's boring doing nothing.'

'I get a good wage. What would you do anyway? An African woman with no qualifications.' He lit a cigarette.

'I can sew. I can dye cloth.'

'No-one wants stuff like that. They buy everything from shops, you daft bugger.'

'There must be something. Maybe cleaning?'

'I don't want you going out cleaning and that's that.'

He switched on the TV. He called and showed her some DVDs he'd bought. 'Soft porn,' he said. 'Let's watch it together.'

She sat with him but she felt ashamed. What were those women doing? How could they do that? Money, she supposed. She went out into the long narrow garden. It was getting warmer. White and pink blossom hung from the trees at the end and yellow daffodils bloomed beside the fence. A blackbird sang its heart out. Who was this man she'd married? It had been so different back home. He had seemed so important, so established, so much fun. Many girls had flirted with him. Sexier, more glamorous girls than her, she thought. She had been shyer, quieter. She cooked the lunches in the hospital kitchen for the overseas medics. He seemed to like her and found excuses to talk to her, to invite her out to the beach or for a meal. But she wouldn't go to the crazy nightclubs he talked about. Even though she was a home girl, neatly dressed, he'd wanted her. She didn't wear make-up or wigs, no weave-ons or straightening. She'd never tried to lighten her skin. She'd looked in the mirror, the eyes were big and slightly slanting, her dark skin shiny in the light, a high rounded forehead, her mouth soft with a touch of red where the fuller upper lip met the lower.

Next leave, there were more videos, nastier. When she knew he was due home she began to feel anxious.

She showed him an advert in the *Gazette*. 'Look, an agency,' she said. 'Regular hours and pay.'

He threw the paper across the room and sulked for the rest of the weekend, complaining about the money she'd spent or the creases in his uniform she ironed.

She had been able to send money for Solomon by doing her own hair and finding the cheapest places for food. She burnt the receipts for the money transfers. But the secrecy and lies made her feel guilty. It's not right to behave this way with a husband; I should talk to him and explain. But he doesn't seem to care about my emotions.

At first he had talked about adopting Solomon but when she raised this he'd say,

'This isn't a good time, petal. We'll talk about it in a few months.'

'Oh Tony,' she said as they lay in bed. 'Please think about it.' She stroked his back and rubbed her body against his, wrapping her leg around him. 'Please.'

'Yeah, yeah,' he murmured as he pressed into her.

He liked having people visit. They praised her food and admired Tony for working in Africa, as they called it. They never used the name of her country, though she corrected them. 'Yeah, we've been to Africa,' some of them said, 'on safari and on the coast. Fabulous beaches. Everyone smiling all the time.'

That weekend he turned up with two friends from work, Brian and Gerry. She cooked, her fingers smelling of garlic, ginger and chilli. After eating, Tony rolled a spliff, passing it to Amina. She shook her head.

'You know I don't like that stuff.'

He pulled a face. 'See how straight my exotic princess is.' The air in the room was suffocating. The men's eyes became bloodshot. Brian sprawled on the squashy sofa, like lying on top of a fat woman.

'Gerry thinks you're beautiful,' Tony said in a soft voice, looking at her closely. 'Your skin is so shiny and you're curvy. He's never had a black woman.'

Amina shifted in her seat and gathered up the dirty plates with trembling hands. Gerry was watching her with a smirk on his round face. She hurried to the kitchen and stacked the dishwasher. What was going on?

Tony leaned against the door jamb.

'We'd like to have some fun. Why don't you come sit with us?'

'Oh you men can talk men things while I clear up.' She forced her mouth into a smile.

He ran his hand over her buttocks while she bent over the dishwasher.

'Be nice to my friends. No harm in having fun.' Something slimy in the tone of his voice.

She ran outside, hiding behind one of the trees. He followed her and gripped her arm. 'We're very liberal in this country. We can make our own rules.'

She spat at him.

'I wouldn't do that Amina. I married you. You'll have to please me if you want to stay or you'll get sent back.'

'What kind of a husband does this? You are a Satan.'

He laughed.

She struggled to get away from his grip, the taste of hate on her tongue. Was he right? Could she be deported? She pulled free and sank down onto the grass, crying until she heard the front door slam and a car start up.

The next time on leave he brought the friends again. She chopped vegetables in a frenzy and nicked her finger. Blood smeared the onions and tears fell into the rice. What had happened to the happy times in Sierra Leone? Sundays on Lakka beach with family picnics, boat trips to waterfalls. Why was it so different here? Where were his parents, any sisters or brothers? He clammed up when she asked about them. No-one worth bothering about, he'd said.

She crouched in a corner of the kitchen but Tony ordered her to get in. Gerry was rushing each forkful into his thin mouth and Brian looked at his plate, embarrassed.

After the meal Tony threatened her again in a whisper. She nodded and pressed her lips together. Gerry followed her up the stairs. His hands were sweaty and his beard glistened with oil from the meat sauce. She could fight back, she knew, but perhaps he would like that. No, she would lie completely still, like a crocodile waiting in the mangrove swamps.

Next leave the same thing happened but this time when Gerry finished he called Brian. Another time Tony stood at the door and watched. He filmed it. Afterwards she went to the bathroom and vomited pieces of stew into the toilet bowl.

She stopped speaking to him. 'Amina's mad at me,' he would say to his kids when they visited, throwing back his head and laughing as she sat in the corner of the kitchen, head bowed, her unbraided hair stuck out in clumps. In the shower she scrubbed her body with nylon. She tried hard to stop herself crying on the phone, talking to her mother and Solomon. In the background she could hear the hubbub from the Freetown streets.

Because she stopped cleaning, cobwebs grew in corners and from ceilings, fragile threads flickering with light. Silvery insects slid out under the skirting boards. The bath grew grey rings. Her bare feet stuck to the kitchen floor.

She'd noticed the spire of a church beyond the estate so she started going to Sunday Mass, longing to speak to someone, but how could she tell the grey-haired priest, even though as she left he always shook her hand gently and smiled.

Tony didn't seem to mind her cold hate, though sometimes, looking around, he'd say,

'Clean up this fucking mess or I'll leave you no more cash.'

One day he leaned over her as she was scouring some pots. 'All my life I've wanted to have a woman who would do what I really wanted. I got you, sweetheart. In your country I was a big man, with beautiful girls coming on to me. But I chose you. Why are you so fucking uptight?'

The sharp kitchen knives stood in a rack nailed to the wall. Amina saw thin pieces of him reflected in the silver blades. She imagined pushing one into his back but Solomon's face came into her head. What would happen if she did such a thing? She looked at the calendar hanging on the wall noting the nine months, nearly a year she'd been here. If she could survive a few more years, surely she would be free of Tony and able to stay? Could she live on quiet hate?

Despite Tony she found work and got up early to clean in a school and then for an old woman. The months passed. How is it possible to block out what is happening, to somehow be present but not be present? She paid them back with sullen resentment and the contempt on her face. She became thin.

One day after work she could not go home. She went to a pub and ordered a drink. A rum. Then more rums. In the toilets she vomited and fell to the floor.

'What's the matter pet?' A woman with scarlet lipstick and piled-up dyed blonde hair leaned over her, breasts spilling out of a sparkly top.

'Yer look rough. What's up?'

The plump face was rough but kind and Amina began sobbing.

'It can't be that bad pet. Is it yer fella?' She knelt down, her skirt sliding up over her thighs.

'Things at home. I can't tell anyone.'

The woman pulled her up. 'You can't shock me, pet. Is he givin' you a hard time? My old fellah used to knock me around something terrible.' She grinned widely to show the row of perfect false teeth.

'I can't take any more.' Amina held her head in her hands.

'You're not from round here, are you?'

Amina shook her head. 'I'm from Sierra Leone.'

'Wherever that is. Look, you probably don't know about refuges.' She offered her a cigarette. Amina shook her head.

'There's a women's refuge in town.' She wrote the telephone number on a paper towel. 'They'd take you in. Help you get your stuff. They helped me. Got me to court to keep the bastard away.'

Amina frowned. 'A refuge. What is that?'

'A secret house like for women who have to get away to be safe.'

'Is it free?'

The woman laughed. 'Course it is. Dunno who pays for it. They'd help you.'

Amina splashed water on her face.

'Why would they help someone like me?'

'Why ever not?' The woman got out her lipstick and redid her mouth.

Amina sighed. It felt too much to explain about her status and the son she'd left behind.

'Give it a try lass.' She slipped the lipstick back into her white handbag. 'And they never change, you know. They promise but they never change.'

Amina nodded. Yes, she would phone. It would be easier to talk to a stranger. It might help and she felt she was losing the strength to continue. Tony would not be back off the rigs for another two weeks. She walked home to the empty house and looked into every room. I came with nothing and I will leave with nothing but what I've earned. She eased out from behind the wardrobe the envelope with her savings in. There's more in the post office. If I have to go home, I won't be going empty-handed. Maybe they will send me back because I've left him but if I tell my story then they might show mercy.

In the morning she phoned the refuge. The voice of the woman who answered was slow and clear. She listened as Amina told her story. She said that they could help, and gave her the address.

'Yes,' said Amina. She felt herself standing taller. In the war, she remembered, her mother had hidden her under furniture when the rebel soldiers attacked and entered the town. Although she was only nine her mother had told her what would happen if the rebels found her. She had had to be brave. They had all been brave. The things that happened did not bear repeating. She would be brave now. If she was refused permission to stay she'd fight that and if she had to go home, well she would face up to it.

Robbie's Friend   Rieve Atkinson

Robbie had always been different, and he'd always been aware of it because of the way he was treated. On his first day at school the other kids had changed his name to "Blobby" and that's how it stayed. They called him other things as well: "Lardy", "Doughboy", "Fat Arse", "Jumbo" and later, at senior school, "Smelly" and "Stink Bomb" were added, which was really unfair. He did sweat a lot but he washed a lot too, then smothered himself in deodorant and body spray to mask any whiffs that might linger. In fact he'd spent most of his pocket money on those things. He clearly remembered the day when he'd asked his mother why he was so fat.

'Robbie, you were born big,' she said, lighting another cigarette to accompany her third glass of sherry, 'and I've told you before, I had to have stitches after you were delivered, which is when I swore I'd never have another kid.'

He felt even worse then, because he thought he might have been the reason why his father had left so long ago. Over the years he'd tried cutting down on food, even not eating solids at all for an awful, painful week, but nothing worked. Then, when he'd been at the Comprehensive for a year and couldn't bear the mockery and bullying anymore, he asked his mother if he could go to the doctor about it.

'You're wasting your time, Son, but if you won't believe me and must hear it from someone else, I'll take you after school tomorrow.'

Doctor Carson, who always smelt strongly of peppermint, peered at him over the top of his glasses, the bridge of which had been repaired with elastoplast.

'Now are you sure, Robbie, that you're not filling up with extra snacks you shouldn't be having?' There it was again, that familiar assumption that he was an uncontrollable glutton. Robbie shook his head in reply.

'Well, we can do some tests and see what they turn up.' The doctor made notes. 'Visit the nurse before you leave and she'll take a few samples. Then come back to me in a fortnight.'

When they returned to the surgery, Doctor Carson told Robbie he had a mild form of Fabry disease which was producing no other symptoms at present, except excess body weight, but it meant that an annual health check was necessary. He also said that it was an inherited condition, which made his mother pipe up defensively.

'Well, he didn't get it from me, Doctor; there's nothing like that on my side of the family!'

'Actually, Mrs Walters, Robbie must have inherited it through the maternal line, as males can only be passed the defective gene via their mothers. You appear to be asymptomatic, fortunately for you. Unfortunately for Robbie, it's incurable, but if he develops other symptoms later in life, he can have a drug called *Fabrazyne* which will control them. Meanwhile, Robbie, you must eat only small portions of low-fat, nutritious food and take extra exercise.'

So Robbie knew from that day that it was hopeless and endless: the condemnation would continue forever and he'd have to live with it. He left school as soon as he could, then a year afterwards, his mother died. She'd been at a neighbour's house playing cards and just fallen from her chair to the floor. A massive heart attack; sudden and final. Her friends organised everything for him and, after the funeral, they helped Robbie deal with the Council officials who moved him into a smaller, one-bedroom flat in a nearby block. His employers at the car spares warehouse allowed him two weeks off for the bereavement, but after that Robbie was glad to get back to his job. He felt valued there, for the first time in his life. He knew the stock number and location of each item better than anyone else, so could be relied on to fulfil the orders quickly. He'd once overheard his manager say that Robbie's efficiency saved the firm time and therefore money. He was known by his workmates as Chubby, but at least that didn't sound quite as gross as some of the other nicknames he'd acquired in the past.

After he'd been at *Auto-Thingz* for four years, something happened that suddenly sharpened his longing to be slimmer. A new delivery driver joined the team. Her name was Mandy, and soon Robbie noticed that she went out of her way to be pleasant to him. She called him by his real name and smiled whenever she saw him. Then after a few weeks, if she was going to the staff kitchen to make a hot drink, she asked Robbie if he wanted one too. Mandy wasn't exactly pretty but she had an open, friendly face, very short, dark hair and expressive brown eyes that always looked directly at him. Robbie liked her and when he was alone, often thought about her, testing himself on how many details of her appearance, mannerisms and habits he could remember. He admired the way she handled the van, particularly when, on returning to the warehouse, she reversed into the loading bay so neatly, quickly and accurately, that it seemed as if the vehicle had become an extension of her body. Unfortunately, he often had difficulty speaking to her, even about quite ordinary things that he could easily have voiced to the other men, so their conversations were rather one-sided, but Mandy was very good at chatting and he hoped that perhaps she hadn't noticed how tongue-tied he was.

Over the months that followed Mandy's arrival, Robbie was aware of his growing longing for her company and of how different and special it felt to have a woman of his own age as a friend, something he'd never experienced before. He'd no idea that he was falling in love, but continually wished that he could improve his appearance for her. Then something happened that gave him hope. It was what his mother would have called 'a fortuitous accident'. Dave, the warehouse forklift-truck driver, regularly bought a girlie magazine called *Nude & Rude,* which he passed on to the other men when he'd finished with it. Robbie was always the last to read it, but that wasn't a disadvantage because it meant he was allowed to keep it. The pictures were alright, but he enjoyed the articles more and the one he was reading now really caught his attention. It was about a morbidly obese woman, who once weighed over twenty-three stones and was desperate to slim down before the health consequences of her size caused illness, or even death. She'd tried different diets but, like him, was eventually told she had a dysfunctional metabolism. Then she'd heard that a tapeworm could be the answer to her problem and discovered it was possible to buy a larva on the internet, swallow it, and wait for it to grow in her intestines where it would feed on whatever she ate, thereby mopping up most of the calories, allowing her to get thinner and thinner. The "before" and "after" photographs illustrated the change in her appearance, showing that she'd become a very slender and attractive woman who now had a lucrative new career as a porn star. At the end of the feature a Russian website was mentioned as the source of the tapeworm.

That evening when he got home from work, before doing anything else, Robbie went online to find the website, which looked legitimate and accepted payment in Euros. He placed an order using *PayPal* and, after his meal, returned to the computer to learn more about tapeworms. He discovered that they could live for up to forty years, fixed by the head to the intestinal wall and, when fully grown, might reach fifty to eighty feet in length but could be killed at any time with a prescription drug called *Praziquantel,* which was reassuring. Two weeks later, Robbie had received and swallowed his encapsulated tapeworm larva, knowing that five to six weeks afterwards it would have matured and started to grow. This, he'd decided, was his only chance of getting down to a normal weight for a man of his age and height: his one opportunity to make himself more attractive to Mandy, so she might start to see him as more than just a friend.

For three months Robbie noticed no difference in himself apart from a mild craving for salty things, and he did make an extra effort to eat less, thinking that this would accustom him to feeling hungry, for when the parasite began absorbing the nutrients that he should be having. Later, he saw some loss of weight every time he checked himself on the bathroom scales. This decrease soon became more rapid, which he presumed was directly due to the continued growth of the worm. Then one night, lying in bed, he felt some movement inside himself. A sort of gentle, undulating sensation, like an internal caress. He imagined it turning, stretching in the moist darkness of his gut, and was surprised at how comforting that felt. As he lay quietly, very aware of this alien living inside him, he decided that it should have a name and chose "Tina", partly because the bit of its Latin name that he could remember was *Taenia,* but mainly after his favourite singer. He knew, from his research on the internet, that tapeworms were hermaphrodites, but it seemed more natural to him that he should be sheltering a female.

At around the same time this happened, Mandy took her annual holiday, camping in France with her friend, Lola. She sent a postcard of the town hall in Quinsac, with greetings to the staff at *Auto-Thingz*, and Robbie began to make a mental note of all the questions he could ask her about the trip, when she returned. He hoped that she'd notice a difference in his size and remark on it, although there hadn't been any comments from the others yet. When Mandy came back to work, she spent the first few days telling everyone about her travels and how she wished she could move to France. Robbie listened carefully to all she said, but unfortunately couldn't ask any of his pre-planned questions because she'd covered all those points herself, several times over. She brought back a fridge magnet with a campsite view for Robbie and told him she was going to learn French, but said nothing about his appearance. At first Robbie put this down to her preoccupation with her holiday, but when he looked in the mirror on his wardrobe door he saw that, despite being over a stone lighter, it didn't really show, even to him. He wondered how much more weight he could lose and how quickly. Unfortunately, he couldn't eat less to help the process along, as he was now constantly hungry and developing a tendency to feel light-headed if he didn't eat often enough.

In another three months Robbie's weight loss had increased to the point where his clothes no longer fitted him and he realised he'd have to get some more. He wasn't used to buying clothes and hated going into shops, where strangers might look at him with either revulsion or pity, so he ordered some tee-shirts and trousers online, purposely selecting dark colours for their slimming effect. When he first went to work wearing his purchases, the others immediately noticed the difference in his appearance and remarked on it. Dave quipped about a possible interest in the opposite sex and said that Chubby must be on the hunt for a girlfriend. Unfortunately he said this in front of Mandy, and Robbie was frozen with embarrassment, so that when she said he looked very nice and asked if he planned to continue with his dieting, all he could do was to nod vigorously at her. His new clothes didn't fit him for that long though, soon beginning to hang from his fast-diminishing bulk, and he knew he'd have to replace them. One morning Mandy asked him, very quietly, if he was ill.

'I know the boys say you're dieting, but you've lost so much weight, Robbie, I wondered if there was something wrong with you.'

He told her that he was fine and that his weight loss was going better than expected. He didn't say his previous size had nothing to do with over-eating because he was afraid that might lead their conversation to doctors, drugs and worst of all, internal parasites. In fact he hadn't been to the surgery for some time, missing his last annual check-up, because he knew there would be questions, then consequences, if he told them the truth. Another important reason for avoiding the place was that, in some areas of his body, his skin was drooping into strange-looking folds, like a series of pale, deflated inner-tubes, so he certainly didn't want to take his clothes off in front of the doctor or nurse.

By the end of August he had lost nine-and-a-half stones but, at his current weight of nineteen stones, he was still determined to lose a bit more. Tina was doing her job well and, as he frequently told her, he was very grateful. The following month Mandy and Lola were going on a city-break to Paris and Robbie decided that this time when she returned, he would ask Mandy if she'd like to go out with him one evening. He thought perhaps a meal and a film would be good. His biggest problem was still the conversation part, although he had begun to feel a lot more relaxed in her company than he used to, so he started making lists of suitable topics and practised talking about them to Tina, filling in Mandy's hypothetical replies as he went along.

It was a wet September morning when Mandy, just back from her trip, brought his coffee to the parts counter and remarked that the weather in Paris had been so much better at this time of year. He listened to her detailed descriptions of the capital's top tourist spots, the shops, atmospheric back-streets, their hotel, the food, the music they'd listened to, and the more he heard the more apprehensive he became. His proposal for an evening out somewhere local seemed less and less appealing, but he knew himself well enough to be sure that if he didn't ask now, he probably never would. She stopped speaking momentarily and he took his chance, with his heart thumping and a trickle of sweat breaking out on his forehead. Mandy seemed surprised, or maybe more accurately, taken aback, and for a few seconds there was an uncomfortable silence. Then she giggled.

'Is this a date Robbie? Because if it is, I don't know what my partner will say.' He felt his jaw drop, then realised he must be looking stunned and really stupid to her right now. 'Lola – my partner. You do know I'm gay don't you, Robbie?' If he'd appeared stunned before, he must now look as though a grand piano had fallen on him from a great height. 'Oh, Robbie,' she stared hard at him, 'you truly didn't have any idea, did you?' He shook his head, hoping fervently that the moisture he could feel pricking his eyes wasn't visible to her. 'I'm so sorry,' she said, 'obviously it's a no-goer, but we can still be friends, can't we? I really am flattered, you know.' With that she turned, gave him a little wave, and walked back towards the despatch area.

He hoped to God she wouldn't tell the others how daft he'd been: he didn't know if he could bear that, already feeling full of embarrassment and leaden disappointment. Mandy liked women, not men. Lola and Mandy. Mandy loved Lola. He'd have to think about that for a while – even though it hurt. When he got home from work, he spoke to Tina about Mandy's revelation and ran it through his mind once again. It'd all been a sort of dream on his part; he knew that now. Yes, he'd lost a lot of weight and thought he looked much better, but not without his clothes on. Naked, he looked decidedly elephantine with all those extra skin folds and he couldn't ever have allowed Mandy to see that. Over the next few weeks, to console himself, he ate as much as he wanted of whatever he fancied and noticed that his rapid weight loss really slowed down to almost nothing, which was fine because it meant he could keep Tina as long as he continued to eat a lot more. Mandy was still friendly towards him, although she always seemed short of time, and thankfully his workmates hadn't found out about his stupid mistake.

At the Christmas party, the manager said that Mandy had something to tell them all and she stood to announce that she was leaving in the New Year to go and live in France with Lola. They'd signed a lease on a small cottage in a village called Saint-Front-la-Riviere. Lola apparently worked as a website designer and could continue to do that, whilst Mandy was going to set up as a self-employed gardener. Afterwards, back in his flat, Robbie wondered why he was feeling more relieved than upset that Mandy was leaving for good, then realised her presence at work would have been a constant reminder of what he couldn't have. He hoped she'd be happy in France but he ... well, he would just carry on doing what he'd been doing for years, except now he wouldn't be alone anymore. He had someone to talk to, to care for: someone who relied on him for her very life and, if the estimates were correct, Tina could be with him until the day he died.

The Settlers

Gerry Webber

My grandmother, Laura, knew what she liked, and what she didn't. She liked *Quality Street* and bottled stout, horse racing on the telly, and two of her grandchildren, including me. Her dislikes were more numerous but certainly included my mother (her only daughter) and my father, who wasn't good enough even for my mum. Apart from helping to bring me into the world, my father had apparently made very little of his life.

'He's a pair of empty trousers,' she liked to remind me. 'Here's ten bob for the weekend. It's a pity your father hasn't got two shillings to rub together.'

Laura was a short woman with spiky features and granite blue eyes. Her face was set in a permanent scowl as if she had recently been stung by a wasp but was determined to pretend that she hadn't, and her lips were habitually pursed and heavily lined, perhaps because she had been a chain smoker for fifty years or more. Her mouth resembled the back passage of an elderly cat, save for the scarlet lipstick which she applied with more vigour than finesse, particularly if she had been drinking in the morning. Her hair was dyed an unnatural shade of chestnut brown and smothered in cheap hairspray. It resembled a cycle helmet. Yet somehow her grey roots always seemed to show through. They looked like frayed wires piercing her scalp, sharp and potentially dangerous. She smelled of toxic chemicals and old cigarettes with a hint of Polo mints and dirty banknotes. She didn't like foreign perfume.

Another thing she didn't like was what she called "the coloureds", although she used the phrase as if she was separating clothes for the weekly wash, and in her defence she was, in her own way, quite egalitarian. She applied the term "coloured" indiscriminately to anyone that she didn't like the look of, and never considered herself to be a racist. She read the Daily Mirror and voted Labour, besides which she was wary of white people too – anyone French or German, for instance. And she didn't trust the Jews. Or the Catholics. Or the Scots.

'Never turn your back on a Jock or a Gyppo,' she used to remind me whenever, as a child, I visited a fair. 'I saw that Lulu on the telly. She's Scottish. Dear God! You call that singing?' My grandmother's conversations were often difficult to follow.

It seemed to me that she went through life like a fairground dodgem, stopping with a jolt only when she ran into someone else, usually on purpose.

Like the dodgems, she had no reverse gear, relying instead on pushing the accelerator hard to the floor whilst spinning the wheel from side to side in the hope that this would allow her to back out of trouble. She was, it seemed, constantly at war with the world, and it was difficult to know if she ever had any real friends, though she had buried three husbands, at least one of whom she claimed to have liked. Perhaps she didn't need proper friends. She had relatives like me instead. So when the Wilson family moved in next door to her, I heard a lot about it.

I must have been about twelve at the time and was staying over for the weekend with one of my less-favoured sisters, Susan. My grandmother drew me aside. 'Here's ten bob for the weekend, and don't tell your sister. Or your father. Or your mother. It's our little secret. Such a shame that father of yours can't find himself a better job.' He worked as a lighting engineer for the General Electric Company.

'Have you seen them?' she asked, peering round the edge of the net curtains.

'They're as black as the devil's armpit, but at least they haven't been playing that Reggie music, not that I've heard anyway.'

'Reggae. It's reggae music,' I corrected her. She ignored me.

'And where did they get a name like Wilson?'

'Jamaica?' I suggested. She wasn't listening, or at least, she wasn't interested in hearing.

'I'm surprised I haven't smelled their cooking yet. They eat some terrible things over there, you know. Goats and all sorts.' She lit another Embassy filter-tipped and blew the smoke from the corner of her mouth, away from the curtains. 'Dreadful smell, apparently. My Fred used to tell a joke about Jamaica, but I forget it now. I've never got along with foreign food. It sets me off something terrible, so it does.' She frowned, and the cat's arse tightened.

Two weeks later, I was there again, on my own this time. I don't know why.

'What's that?' I asked, looking at the moist, dark cake on the front-room table.

'It's ginger cake,' she said. 'Home made.'

Now this was unusual for my grandmother, not only because she professed not to like ginger, which "disagreed" with her, but also and mainly because she refused to bake anything herself. Her kitchen was merely a place where the tins and packets that she retrieved from the larder were opened and arranged on dinner plates or put into bowls prior to serving things up in the front room, occasionally warmed-through. 'If God had meant us to cook, he wouldn't have invented the Co-op,' she told me. The only exception was anything that could be prepared in the deep-fat fryer, which otherwise sat on the stove as a handy container for off-white lard.

'It looks good. Where did it come from?' I was angling for a slice or two.

'Theresa brought it round, on her way to church,' she said, avoiding my gaze.

'Theresa?'

'The little girl next door. Lovely manners, and she dresses very smartly. That sister of yours could take a few lessons from Theresa, I'll tell you that for nothing. Your Susan's no better than she should be. I sometimes wonder if your mother pays any attention to what that girl wears.' My grandmother was a fountain of gratuitous advice.

I was back the following Sunday with my youngest sister, Louise, who had just turned five, and was too young to have yet fallen foul of my grandmother. Susan was camping with the Brownies and my parents were redecorating the bathroom.

'I don't know why that father of yours doesn't get a man in to do it properly. He made a terrible mess of the back room. There again, I don't suppose he can afford it. Not on his wages. I don't know what she sees in him. But that's between you, me and the gatepost.' She looked at me conspiratorially and tapped the side of her nose. 'Here's ten bob' she said. 'Don't tell your mother. Or your father. Now, what shall we have for lunch?'

It was unusual to be offered a choice. It was normally cold ham, fresh from the tin, and salad accompanied by a few plain crisps.

'What is there?' I asked.

'Well, there's ham ... or there's Jerky chicken. It's a bit spicy but ... Victoria made it. Theresa's mother,' she added by way of an explanation. My grandmother searched in the pocket of her blue nylon pinny and retrieved a half-finished packet of Embassy. She lit another cigarette, for something to do. 'They're very nice people when you get to know them,' she said, inhaling. 'Very religious, which is good, although I can't be doing with our church these days. That awful vicar with the bald-patch? I'm sure he's a pansy. Have you seen him? He looks like a Jew!' I said nothing for a moment or two.

'I'll have the ham, please.'

When Mr. Fletcher moved in to the house next to my grandmother, on the opposite side from the Wilsons, I thought at first that my grandmother's social life was on the up. Like her, he enjoyed horse racing and drinking, though he gambled, which she didn't, and he mostly drank bitter, usually from tins, and sometimes in his front garden, which consisted of little more than a few concrete slabs separating his front door from the pavement.

'Well, he's not Jewish,' I said to my grandmother a few weeks after Mr Fletcher had arrived, 'and he's not Scottish. Do you like him?'

Mr. Fletcher was a broad man with small eyes the colour of cigarette ash. He had dark hair cut so short that it looked like a stain on his head and puffy lips that were strangely feminine. He walked as if he were crossing the deck of a ship at sea, and his arms hung slightly away from his sides. He appeared to be a man of few words.

'Alright, son?' he said to me one day as I sat on the front step of my grandmother's house, enjoying the last of the summer sun. My parents were decorating their bedroom and my sisters had chosen to stay with my other granny for some reason. I nodded at him in what I thought was a grown-up form of response, and we remained together in companionable silence, apart from the occasional sound of him slurping beer from a tin.

Then Theresa appeared, wearing a short yellow dress with red sandals. She was carrying a small tupperware box with food inside. I liked Theresa, though we knew each other mainly by sight. Our relationship mostly involved smiling at one another while my grandmother talked.

'It's for your granny,' she said. 'Banana bread.'

I turned to call for my grandmother but realised that she was already in the hallway not very far behind me, looking at herself in the mirror. She was wearing a pretend fur coat, despite the weather, and touching up her lipstick.

'I'm just nipping out to the shops for some cigarettes and a ginger wine,' she announced, tottering towards the front door on her high heels. She never left the house without make-up and had no time for women that went shopping in housecoats and slippers. According to my grandmother, you could tell a lot about a person from the way that they looked, which was how she knew that the man who lived two doors down didn't like women, apparently.

'Oh, thank you, darling,' she said to Theresa. 'And thank your mummy, too.'

'They're alright when they're little, aren't they?' It was Mr Fletcher, joining the conversation uninvited. His voice was slightly slurred. 'When they're kids, I mean, like this one.' He tipped his beer can vaguely in Theresa's direction but spoke as if she wasn't there. Theresa looked up at the adults, unsure if she could leave when she was the subject of a conversation. 'It's like animals, isn't it? Wild animals. Lions and tigers and ... gorillas and things. They're cute when they're babies but not when they grow up. Know wha' I mean?' My grandmother looked as if she was about to say something. But she didn't. So Fletcher continued, 'It's like bananas. They're fine in the jungle but they just don't suit the weather over 'ere, if you get my drift. They're better where they came from, eh Laura?'

Mr. Fletcher stared aimlessly across the road and took another sip of his beer. Theresa looked confused and a little frightened, as if she'd been accused of breaking a rule that she didn't understand. I waited for Granny to say something.

My grandmother inhaled noisily and drew herself up to her full height, pulling her overcoat tight against her wiry frame. Then she crouched in front of Theresa and reached into the pocket of her fake fur coat. 'Here's ten bob,' she said. 'Don't tell your mother.'

‖Sophia

On the bridge a young woman hugs herself. It is a desolate night in the dead of winter. She wears only a thin, short dress – no defence against the cold easterly funnelling up the Tyne. Her bare arms are discoloured by bruises of every hue: faded green and yellow to livid purple. She stares at the changing colours of the Millennium Bridge and the faux-Manhattan skyline of the Sage. Lights shine for other people, she thinks.

When she escaped once before, they smashed her toes, warning it was her last chance. They control everything she does, and say that the police are in their pockets too.

'Yamas!' her father raises his glass. They all chorus in response, 'Yamas!' The supper is a success, much to her mother's relief. The unexpected arrival of Sophia's cousin Nicos alone would not have disturbed her, but he is accompanied by his smooth, handsome friend Theo – and this has thrown her into a panic. Throughout the meal Theo peppers Sophia's mother with compliments and she responds with modest smiles. He finishes by wiping up the sauce rimming his bowl with a hunk of bread, gripping his stomach, and declaring the meal as good as any served in his restaurant. Her mother beams with pride. Sophia also observes a change of expression in her father's flushed face.

'You must tell us of this restaurant, Theo,' he says.

'I can do better than that. You can view it on this video clip if you like,' he replies and proffers his phone.

'Look at this, Mama!' her father exclaims, 'It's named after him too.'

By the time Sophia – tired of listening to drunken conversation – makes her excuses to go to bed, the glasses have been refilled several times. She curls up and thinks about the stranger who has charmed her parents, and how odd it was that Nicos remained so quiet throughout the evening.

Next morning at the breakfast table Sophia is shocked when her parents tell her they've accepted, on her behalf, a waitressing job at the restaurant owned by Theo. She pleads with her father that she doesn't want to leave the village.

'I'll be homesick and miss you, and my friends too of course.'

But he dismisses her concerns, 'You are nineteen. It's time you earned a living. You can live with Nicos until you get settled. He has done well there and will look after you.'

'Don't I need some papers?' she asks.

'Theo says he will sort that for you. He's a businessman and knows the ways of the world. There is a special work permit for us exiles in the minority zone. This is a great opportunity for you, Sophia. Here in Albania we are the North Korea of Europe but our homeland is recovering. You could see that the restaurant is doing well. Just think, you will be able to send money home to help us feed your brother and sisters.'

Sophia feels everything is happening too quickly, that something isn't quite right, but there is nothing she can say to convince her parents, seduced by the prospect of her earnings boosting the family budget.

Her father says, 'It is settled then, you can go with them when they leave at the end of the week.'

A few days later as they all approach the border in Theo's limousine, Sophia sitting quietly in the back is preoccupied by the image of her mother weeping and waving as she left home. The sight of armed guards at the entrance to a barbed wire fenced encampment sweeps those thoughts from her mind.

Theo, seeing her troubled face in the rear-view mirror tells her, 'They are refugees, mainly Syrians, but also Iraqis, and North Africans too. The authorities in Greece are happy to let them continue their travels into Albania instead of dealing with their requests for asylum.'

Sophia understands and nods. Theo continues, 'The border guards are more concerned about those hordes than individuals going the other way.'

Even from the road Sophia sees the camp is overcrowded with tent after tent and makeshift shelters of flapping plastic sheets, stretching out as far as she can see. There are ragged, thin children begging at the roadside beside their harrowed parents. She says, 'Oh, these poor people look so desperate.'

'You wouldn't want to be one of them,' says Theo as he turns off the highway. For a few miles they bump along a rough track. When at last the car rejoins a metalled road, it is evident from the road signs, they are now in Greece. Sophia wonders why Theo took her passport when he intended to avoid border controls.

The streets of Athens are busy and crowded. Sophia recognises the restaurant, but when the car stops only Nicos gets out, saying to Theo, 'Okay, we are quits now, right?'

A sickening grin spreads across Theo's face, 'Yes, my friend, your debt is cancelled.'

A heavily built man slips into the back seat beside Sophia. 'This is Sandro,' says Theo, 'You will learn to do what he tells you, first time of asking.'

Sophia opens her mouth to scream but Sandro's huge hand forces it shut. She grabs the handle of the car door – it's locked. Sandro smashes her head against a window.

When Sophia recovers consciousness she is lying on a bed in a darkened room. Five barely dressed young women are looking at her. One of them, wearing a flimsy negligee, offers Sophia a glass of water and asks her name. She tells Sophia, 'I have to show you how to dance. They want to set you to work tomorrow.'

'I want to get out of here. There's been some mistake. I am here to waitress in the restaurant,' replies Sophia. She sees her handbag lying open, its contents spilled on the floor, 'Where's my phone?'

Sophia sees the raised eyebrows of the other girl and feels stupid for even asking.

Within a week Sophia is on 'the menu' at a seedy nightclub, alongside lurid pictures of the other girls variously posed in baby-doll outfits, nurses' uniforms, wearing fishnet stockings, or leather corsets. Sophia has learned always to smile at customers, how to gyrate, to distinguish between the punters who only want to buy drinks and watch her perform and those who will demand sex. She has learned quickly – after one beating from Sandro.

From conversations with the other girls, she discovers the restaurant is just a front used to launder the money gained from the illicit club across the road. She thinks, if only her parents had listened. But they'd swallowed all Theo's lies: his perfect lies. As for Nicos, no matter how desperate he was and whatever the hold Theo had on him, his betrayal of family was even worse.

At the end of each night's work she is locked in the room with the other women. She dreams of one thing – escape. But each morning she awakens to the nightmare of her existence. One day she sees Theo and screams at him, begging him to release her.

He says, 'I will send your parents the photographs and tell them you have brought dishonour to their family, that Nicos and I tried to keep you at the restaurant but instead you have chosen this life.'

'They won't believe you,' she cries.

'Well then perhaps they will meet with an accident,' he says, 'Sandro would like to visit your village.'

Sophia loses her sense of time. The days merge into each other, her life reduced to a struggle for survival. She discovers a way of mentally closing down when she is with a punter. She wonders what her parents know. Why have they done nothing? Has Theo been sending texts from her phone to reassure them? Her hopes of rescue fade.

One night the girls whisper about a police raid and Sophia feels her heartbeat quicken with hope. Suddenly, Sandro bursts through the door of their room, shouting, 'We are selling our stock!' grabs Sophia by her hair and drags her to his car. As they speed away to the airport Sandro tells her she must not speak to anyone throughout the flight or he will kill her. Before they go through security Sophia feels the hypodermic needle pierce her arm. The flight becomes a hazy memory of sleepiness, hissed threats and an air stewardess smiling her practised smile, somehow oblivious to Sophia's pleading eyes. She holds her passport briefly at the control before it is taken from her again.

She is taken to a squalid flat, above a massage parlour – the front for the brothel. The other women there have been trafficked into the country too. Sophia's English is limited and communication is made even more difficult by the range of nationalities. There are two Romanians, two Nigerian teenagers and a Vietnamese woman who mimes painting her fingernails – she thought she was coming for a job in a nail bar.

A ferocious, thick-set man with a neck like a bulldog and a shaven head shouts at Sophia. He says he is Vic, her pimp. She understands a little of what he says – that she owes him money for the airfare and she must work to repay the debt. And so the abuse resumes, punter after punter, night after night. Her understanding of English improves. Vic tells her that she's overstayed her visa and is now an illegal alien; that Albanians never get asylum, and she is stuck here. When Vic offers her drugs, she takes them – anything to numb the pain.

It is obvious that many of the men guess her true situation: that this is happening against her free will, but they don't care. Some punters are weirdos, others violent. One man is different; he is old, probably over sixty she thinks. Joe, one of her regulars, is a lonely widower who just likes to talk to her. He is one of a few clients who use the escort service, and she goes to his home. Sometimes he takes her out. It is a relief when he books her to spend an evening at his home, knowing he will not hurt her. She only needs to nod and smile at appropriate intervals. When she is taken over the Tyne Bridge to his house in Gateshead, by Vic or one of his hard men, it is a rare opportunity for her to see the outside world. She thinks the weather in Newcastle is awful. It is so cold, and windy. Yet there is something about the city that she likes – the riverside.

Tonight there is no one available to drive her to Joe's house, so Vic calls a taxi. The driver taking her to the house says he will be back at twelve o'clock to pick her up, but he arrives twenty minutes late.

'Are y'alreet bonny lass?' he asks on the return journey.

Sophia is filled with dread at the prospect of returning to the flat.

'Just drop me off here,' she says, surprised by her own impulsiveness.

'What here, at this time of night?' he replies, pulling over onto the deserted slip road leading to the Tyne Bridge .

Over the radio there is a call from the operator asking the driver where he is because she's received a query about the whereabouts of the passenger. Hearing this, Sophia slams the car door and starts to run along the footway of the bridge. She stops. Where is she running to? There is nowhere for her to go, nor to hide. Vic has told her this often enough. This is madness. Vic will kill her when he catches her.

Sophia looks out at the lights along the river for a few moments, then clambers onto the top of the railings, trembling with cold and fear. To steel herself to end the short, sad span of her life she thinks of the punters – their beery breath and stale sweat.

Her vision is blurred by tears. Wiping her eyes she is shocked by firm hands gripping her shoulders.

'I knew something was wrong; yee need help.'

She turns to face her saviour – the taxi driver. A spark of hope fires inside her.

It is Sunday morning. Sophia looks up at the Tyne Bridge from the quayside market. Sometimes she experiences a flashback of the terror of that winter night six months ago, but today the blue July skies lift her spirits. When she's busy the memories recede for a while, like in the restaurant when the shift is over, they clean up and she sits down with her workmates to chat at a table. The talk is always about the customers: the noisy drunks celebrating, the good tippers, couples who barely speak or the other short dramas they observe playing out each night. It is later, alone in bed, that dark thoughts return – of fear and rage, the bitterness at her cousin's treachery. Vic was charged, but she worries whether he will actually be convicted or if she'll always be looking over her shoulder. She doubts that anyone else will be brought to justice.

The lies spread in her village mean she cannot go back. In the future, perhaps it may be possible. Her shattered youth cannot be restored but each day she will strive to reclaim her life and value the precious blessing of a free existence. If she gives up, then Vic, Theo and the others who treated her as worthless will have won. She remembers the forlorn faces of the refugees in the border camp, who had no hope, and feels she also owes it to them to grasp the chances that asylum gives her.

She threads her way through the crowd, admires the pictures for sale at one stall and moves on. People are smiling and laughing as they, too, browse in the market. Her best friend, Josie, bargains with a stall-holder and presses a framed picture of all the bridges across the Tyne – Sophia's favourite local scene – into her hands. Sophia is touched by the gesture, content to be part of this – the rhythm of everyday life.

Tacet

Judith Wall

It was while chatting to my nephew, Chet, about his history degree course, that it dawned on me that the whole 2028 thing was being suppressed. I'd asked him, just out of interest, how that time was presented in school, and he said that he'd never come across it in any of his studies.

'But you know what I'm talking about?' I asked, 'You must have heard your parents or grandparents talking about it.'

'You mean that time they changed the calendar for a short while? That's hardly something that needs dwelling on, is it?'

He'd been born in 2057, twenty-nine years after the event, and seemed ignorant about it. Later that week I asked his mother, my sister Oak, whether she had ever discussed that time with Chet.

'No,' she said. 'That time's TACET.'

I must have looked puzzled.

'It's a musical term meaning silent that we use in the Civil Service to mean that if nothing is recorded in any way about a subject, it will be forgotten eventually. Of course people talk, but they all die off, and then future generations' versions of events will vary and develop an air of myth. They'll come across no information whatsoever on the subject.

'But how on earth can that be enforced?' I asked. 'It's impossible. Think of all the people who worked on the time factor element, for a start.'

She made two gestures: she rubbed her thumb against her finger tips to suggest money payments and then mimed the slitting of her throat. She shrugged.

'You'll find nothing, Ash; no archives are available.'

'But what does it matter anyway? What's the point of hushing it up?'

'Posterity. The powers that be don't want to be looked back on as ignorant.'

We're twins, born in '36, eight years after the event. I remember our parents talking about it, but they're gone now, killed in a floater craft accident when we were twenty.

'Do you remember Dad talking about— ?' I began, but she drew her finger across her lips to seal them.

I took Oak's word for it that nothing was available on the subject, and began, in my own quiet way, to record the spoken memories of people who had been alive in 2028. I went down to the Pleasure Palace, where most sixty- and seventy-year-olds are to be found during the day. They were eager to talk about themselves, as most people are. I recorded their voices on the memo bean in my ear, and copied them on to the retro coil when I got home, just in case.

1.4.2078 Baxter Corrigan aged 69

Yeah, are you nuts? Of course I remember it all. It was a crazy time. We still had television in those days, and for six months or so, we had been introduced to the idea that the speed at which the Sun and Earth were moving away from each other was increasing at a rate that hadn't been predicted. Instead of the fifteen centimetres a year that had been the norm, all of a sudden they're telling us that it had already got to the point where they were considering adding a day to the year. Hey, did you know that when the Moon was newly formed, the days on Earth were only five hours long? Yeah? Well, eventually, they tell us that they're going to add an extra day on to April. Why April? Who the heck cares? So they add this extra day on, see. They tell us on 24th April, so we've just a week to get used to the idea. Just an extra day, nothing to get excited about. Same as you get in a leap year, like we'd had that February.

Well, folks started thinking about what it meant. If the Sun and Earth were moving away from each other at a faster rate, how long before the Earth's orbit went wonky? How long before we were all doomed? People thought they'd better make the most of the time they had left. It had a crazy effect on us all.

What's that? Oh sorry, I got to go for my retread now. Maybe catch you later.

1.4.78 Myrtle Jenkins aged 67

When the 31st April arrived, I don't know, it was like everyone was gripped by a feeling of devil-may-care. People were organising parties and concerts. The weather was beautiful, like a perfect summer's day. The Prime Minister had been on TV, telling us all that it was just an ordinary day, a working Monday. Everyone who could was taking the day off work, and people like me who were still at school were pulling a sickie. My friend, Sunnie, and I went down to the concert in the park. Well when we got there, I was stoked to spot two A1 boys who we hadn't seen before. We worked our way over so that we were right beside them and started chatting them up. Well it wasn't something that we would normally do, but we just didn't care. Well, after the concert we went down to the hill beside the river where the long grass is. Ha! You'd have laughed if you'd seen it. The bank was covered with couples locked together. Me and my boy, Argo, could hardly find a place to sit. Luckily the grass was so long that once we were down, we didn't notice anyone else. Anyway, the upshot was that by the time I left the hill, I was a bit pregnant, and so was Sunnie, and as it turned out, hundreds of other women were the same bit pregnant that night.

2.4.78 Hildebrand Fitzsimmons aged 75

It was a perfect day. Hardly a breath of wind stirred. I'd been living with Romeo for four years by then, and to be honest, it wasn't going anywhere. I was keen to have a baby, but Romeo wasn't having any of it – literally. Anyway, there was something about that day. It filled me full of longing, a yearning for something. You could say that spring fever got me. There was an ache all through me and I couldn't stand being in the house. Romeo had gone to work. Being a health worker, he couldn't take random days off, so I went out and wandered aimlessly about, feeling a bit sorry for myself. I went down to the beach. There was this gorgeous fella leaning against the railing on the promenade, sort of eyeing me up. Soon as I caught his eye, this great wave of lust washed through me and my face turned bright red. He was bold, I can tell you. Held out his hand and pulled me against him, whispered something dirty in my ear and asked me to go to the hotel with him. You'll think me awful, but I went, didn't even ask his name. We spent all afternoon in that hotel, and I tell you I've never known anything like it. Lust, that's all it was, and when I came out, I can tell you I knew darn well that I was pregnant.

I could include at least twenty more stories similar to this one, from women who had been young at the time. All include lust and pregnancy. I needed to find some older people to talk to, who still had all their marbles. I made enquiries at the home for retired professionals.

10.4.78 Campbell Black aged 90

It was pretty scary stuff all right. No one knew how the rate of acceleration would increase. I was working in aviation at the time, and we got to hear a bit more than the news programmes told us. The science buffs were really worried that the culprit was the influence of dark matter. Hell, are we much further on now with our understanding of it? They were really frightened. On the 31st April, the young folk seemed to be gripped by a kind of recklessness. My wife and I spent the day at work as usual, though we both said that we felt restless all day. Our kids went to school as if it was an ordinary Monday. It was just those between the ages of 17 and 27 who were strongly affected, but although the guys were up for partying, the women were more consumed by lust. You'll be hard pushed to find a man who said he'd had sex on that day, so the question has to be, who the hell were the daddies? Now there are four more important things:

1. *In Britain alone, every woman who had sexual intercourse that day became pregnant.*
2. *No babies were born on 31st April 2028. How come? It's a mystery put down to coincidence.*
3. *The events of 1st May.*
4. *All the babies conceived on 31st April, and only the babies conceived on 31st April, were born a month early on 31st December2028. Not one of them was born in the next year.*

Now if you'll excuse me, I need to rest. My brain may be healthy, but my body is weary.

16.4.78 Farquhar Ferguson aged 87

You've come to the right place if you want to know what happened on 1st May 2028. I was a seismologist. I was at work that day, and I can tell you, there was no earthquake. That was the official line and we went along with it in order to keep our jobs. Well now, I was in the canteen, looking out at the ornamental garden and pond when I experienced a powerful sensation of everything being sucked up, shaken, squashed, rocked, knocked over, suffocated, any words you can think of to describe a sudden, overpowering force that knocks you for six. All this was accompanied by a noise similar to a soundtrack being played backwards very loudly. Outside, the water in the pond had formed one large, motionless wave, the trees were bent over and the sky had turned purple. This lasted for what seemed like two or three minutes, and then the soundtrack slowed down to an unintelligible deep sort of voice and stopped. We were all pretty shaken up, but our instruments had registered no seismic activity. People were easily convinced that there'd been an earthquake, and seemed happy to ignore the fact that it had been worldwide. As long as they were ok, huh? You know how people are.

I'd made a lot of progress. During the first half of April I managed to speak to twenty people. I made two coils: one with all the interviews I'd recorded, and this one which avoids needless repetition. I spent the next nine days interviewing people at clubs and care homes, being told the same stories over and over of lust and doubts about paternity. Oddly enough, no couples had split up over it. The men all accepted the responsibility of parenthood. Then one day, I heard a different story in the waiting area of the arthritis clinic.

25.4.78 Lilla Greenwood aged 77

I was a trainee midwife in those days. I was at work when what they called the earthquake occurred. People died, you know. They hushed that up as much as they could. They didn't die from buildings collapsing or falling through craters or anything like that, they just died. When everything went back to normal, lots of people were dead. Anyway, to move on to the 31st December. It was all hands on deck that day. They had to bring in extra people to cope with the demand, but as far as I remember, it went smoothly and all the babies were healthy. I remember going home on the morning of the New Year and listening to the news. They were saying that scientists were beginning to think that they'd miscalculated the timing of the Sun and Earth moving away from each other. By 1st April, they were saying that they'd probably cancel the extra day and go back to thirty days. But if I were you, I'd go and speak to a guy called Professor Sylvester. He's in the hospice now, but his brain's still sharp. There's not much that he doesn't know. Don't tell anyone that I put you on to him.

28.4.78 George Sylvester aged 92

I've thought long and hard about what I'd say if someone like you turned up. I was an astronomer, top notch. I'm one of the many who received huge payoffs. We signed official secrecy documents and lived in luxury. It's hypocritical of me to tell the truth now, but I worry about what is to come. With the end so near, it doesn't seem right to take the truth to the grave, and I don't have any offspring they can threaten.

As is always the case, someone recorded the noises that were heard during the earthquake. As suspected, it was being played backwards, and when it was reversed, a deep voice was saying very slowly, "A war-ning, a war-ning." Not long afterwards, it was discovered that the Earth was at the same distance from the Sun as it had been a year ago and that the rate of acceleration had returned to what was considered normal. It wasn't that things had gone backwards. No children looked younger or anything like that, but something had been reversed. Governments were worried that the truth about the recording would get out, triggering panic, religious extremism, or a scramble for supremacy among the major powers. In a unique display of global harmony, all of the world's governments sent representatives to a summit where they agreed on the TACET approach. A series of rumours and counter-rumours were spread to confuse the public as to the truth, and so it's gone on.

I left him at that point as he was exhausted, but resumed the interview the next day.

29.4.78 Interview continued:

The thing was, the government and scientists were terrified. Where had the voice come from? Was it the voice of God? What if it had come from dark matter? The world seemed to have been reset at a distance from the Sun that was safer, better, but what had put it there? They'd rather not know and they'd rather not be seen to not know. This head-in-the-sand solution has gone on for the last fifty years.

There's one aspect of the story that I haven't mentioned, though. All the babies conceived on that one and only 31ˢᵗ April are highly intelligent, kind-hearted, hardworking leaders in their many, varied fields. This isn't made much of, but if you do your research you'll find doctors, scientists, writers, or in some countries, farmers, teachers and nutritionists. None are connected to the military or religion or politics. I keep thinking about their political absence. Don't they want to be part of TACET? Are they keeping away from negative influences, or is there something else? All of them are involved with helping people. They form a close-knit group both nationally and internationally. They communicate in an unremarkable way and hold get-togethers every 30ᵗʰ April.

What's that? Yes, the Hilton I believe. Oh, and before you go, I came to the conclusion that all the people who died in the earthquake were villains, bullies or wasters, but that's too difficult to prove. But then the whole thing is unbelievable.

I went down to the Hilton the next evening and sat in the lobby as they arrived. They all looked younger than their forty-nine-and-a-bit years, and seemed to glow with a healthy radiance. I saw that famous scientist, Heradim Tate and that face transplant doctor, Cortauld Baines. There was no chance of being a fly on the wall of course, but I did manage to bribe a young waiter into wearing a memo bean.

Rocco Brookes aged 23

They were talking about their fiftieth birthdays when I went in, just in ones and twos, like. Then I had to go and get the aperitifs, but I think I got all the important bits when I came back.

I went home and listened to what was on the bean. I heard someone tap on a glass for silence, then:

This is it. I've been in touch about what will happen in December, and I've had a message back from them already. It says, "Warning not investigated, *heeded or understood. Your fathers and their teams will arrive on 31st December, when you reach the age of wisdom. Stand by to help them. There are worries that we have left it too late, but the date has long been set. The people will be rebraced. This planet is too valuable to lose."*

I feel so sick. What on earth is going to happen?
Who can I tell? Oh help. Help us all.
Where the hell are these fathers coming from and ... what on earth does 'rebraced' mean?

Zap, zap!

Gerald Cole

Zap! I go as we ride along. *Zap, zap, zap!*

'What are you doing, Baby?' asks Maya.

'I'm zapping,' I tell her. 'I'm zapping people.' *Zap, zap, zap!* I go.

'Don't do that,' says Daro. He's driving. 'Don't zap people.'

'But I've got a zapper,' I tell him. 'It's for zapping. See?' I stick it out the window. *Zap, zap!* I go

'You shouldn't do that, Baby,' says Maya. 'Zapping's not nice.'

'But I've got a zapper.' I frown. 'It's a good zapper.' I show them. *Zap! Zap!*

There's a noise behind us. Someone's whooping and wailing. It's a new noise. I don't know it. It makes Daro angry. He makes a big harrumph. We slow down. We stop.

'Why are we stopping?'

'Just be quiet, Baby,' says Maya. She looks scared.

A big light blinks behind me. I twist round.

A car has stopped behind us. It's blinking at us.

I feel scared.

A man hits Daro's window. I jump. He's right outside. He's all in black.

Maya turns round. She touches me. 'Don't worry, Baby. Everything's alright.'

Daro makes his window go down. He says to the man in black: 'Can I help you, officer?'

The man pushes his head inside. He looks round. 'I saw something pointing out of a window,' he says. He sees me.

I squeeze back into my seat.

'What's that in your hand, son?'

I shake my head.

'Just my kid's toy,' says Daro. 'That's what you must have seen.'

The man just looks at me. I don't like him looking at me. 'Is that right, son?' he says.

Maya is looking at me too. She nods.

'It's my zapper,' I say, very quietly.

'Can I see it?'

He smiles. It's not like Maya and Daro smile. But it makes me feel better. I show him my zapper.

'Well, that's pretty cool,' says the man. 'Some kind of space gun, is it?'

'No,' I say. 'It's my zapper.'

'You gonna zap something for me, then?'

Maya and Daro's faces go funny. But the man is still smiling. I grin.

'Baby!' Maya and Daro shout together.

But I'm already turned round. I push my zapper out the window. I zap the blinking car behind us.

The blinking stops. I turn back. Nobody's smiling. Everybody looks scared. The man in black looks really, really scared.

'Where'd my cruiser go?' he says. His voice sounds funny. 'What did you just do?'

Things are not right. Everyone is looking at me. I'm really scared. I start to cry.

'OK,' the man says loudly. 'Everybody out— '

He jumps back so fast he bangs his head on the top of the window.

'Baby,' says Daro quietly. 'Be a good boy. Zap him.'

I zap him.

'Good boy,' says Daro.

I'm crying hard now. Maya turns round. She strokes my head.

'It's OK, Baby. Let me have this now.'

She takes away my zapper.

'You said I shouldn't zap people,' I say.

'I know, Baby,' says Maya. She's looking at my zapper.

She touches the dial on the side. The one I'm not supposed to touch.

'What's the setting?' says Daro.

'Two over four,' says Maya.

'I set it at neutral!'

'Don't blame, Baby!' Maya looks angry. She turns to me. 'You didn't touch the dial, did you, Baby?'

'No,' I say quietly. I don't want to look at her.

But Maya is looking back at the zapper. 'This dial is so easy to move.'

Daro makes a loud sound with his nose. He starts driving.

'They'll all be back in a day or so,' says Maya. 'They won't remember a thing.'

'This is a class four world,' says Daro. 'These primitives barely know which way is up. They won't just pop into stasis for a few hours. They'll be lucky to come back at all!'

'Well, perhaps you shouldn't have brought a zapper with us.'

'Well, perhaps we shouldn't be driving around with a kid!'

I start to cry. I don't like shouting. It frightens me.

Daro goes quiet. Then he goes: 'Aaagh!' He stamps on the car floor. The car squeals and stops. I scream.

'What are you doing?' says Maya.

Daro throws open the door. He jumps out the car. He stamps on the ground. I scream.

'You're terrifying him!' shouts Maya. 'Stop it!'

She jumps out the car. She runs at Daro. She slaps him.

I stop screaming. Some things are too frightening for screams.

Daro stops stamping. He talks quietly.

'It's a piddling little planet no one gives a bloated falloon about, but it's our first First Contact mission. We only get one! Get it wrong and we'll never go offworld again. We may as well bury ourselves here. It's our decision to make. And it doesn't need the distraction of Baby!'

Maya is very angry. I've never seen her so angry. This is bad.

'He's our first full-term fledgling here. Do you expect me to abandon him?'

Daro sighs. He looks at the ground. Then he looks up.

'How many fledglings do you pod in season?'

Maya's face goes hard. 'What exactly are you saying?'

'Is it two, would you say, or three thousand?'

Maya doesn't speak.

'Actually,' says Daro, 'I think it's been almost four before now, hasn't it?' He shakes his head. 'Don't get me wrong. Baby's a good kid – when he's not zapping people. But, let's face it, he's not exactly unique, is he?'

Maya's eyes go teeny tiny. I'm scared. She turns and looks at me with her teeny tiny eyes. 'Baby,' she says, 'fetch the zapper.'

'Oh come on— ' says Daro.

I look between the front seats. The zapper's on Maya's seat. If I stretch I can almost reach it.

'Baby!' Daro calls. 'You leave that thing alone. You hear me?'

I have to stretch and stretch. My fingers touch it. 'Got it!' I call.

'Maya!' Daro shouts. 'You're playing stupid games! This is where it all stops!'

He jerks open the car door. I start. His face is all big and red.

'Give me that, Baby!' he shouts. He jumps at me. I scream. The zapper goes *zap*. I can't breathe. I try to cry. I want to. I can't.

'There, Baby.' Maya gets into the car. She pulls me onto her lap. She takes the zapper out of my hand. She cuddles me. It's good.

'Don't worry, Baby. It's all over now. Maya's here.'

In a while she puts me in the other front seat. It's nice up front. She smiles at me. I smile back. The car moves off.

'Will Daro come back?' I say.

'I expect,' says Maya. 'Don't worry about that.' She gives me another smile. 'We won't be lonely.'

'We won't?'

'Soon,' says Maya, 'you're going to have lots and lots of brothers and sisters. Would you like that?'

I think about it. 'Will they play with me?'

'Of course.'

I smile. Then I think something else. 'Will they want to play with my zapper?'

'Oh no,' says Maya. 'They'll have their own zappers.'

'Really?'

'Oh yes. We're going to be staying here for a while, Baby, so we're all going to need zappers. Lots and lots of zappers.'

'Can I play with mine now?'

She looks at me. Then she looks down at the zapper. She touches the dial on the side. The one I'm not allowed to touch. She pushes it all the way over. 'Why not?' She gives the zapper to me. 'We're going to have to make room for all your new playmates, aren't we?'

I smile. The road ahead is getting busy. There are lots of people. Maya makes the window go down.

Zap! I go, *zap, zap, zap!* I laugh. Maya laughs. 'It's a good zapper,' I say.

'Yes, Baby,' says Maya. 'It is.'

BIOG NOTES

Fiona Ritchie Walker writes poetry and short fiction. For many years she travelled the globe visiting fair trade producers and artisans. Her story – which took shape during a month's writing fellowship at Hawthornden Castle, Scotland – is dedicated to all those who helped stop her from becoming a full-blown Rosan.

Noreen Rees' short stories have been published in various anthologies including *Mudsnake* in *Platform* (Nexus/New Writing North) and *The Installation* in *Cold Iron* (IRON Press). She has also had several plays performed, including *Not Some Kind of Sideshow* (NTC*),* and two children's books published. She has worked on several community projects.

Andrew Sutherland began writing six years ago and enjoys creating darkly offbeat short stories, sometimes with a touch of gallows humour. He cites the work of Michael Moorcock, Gene Wolfe, Philip K Dick and J G Ballard as major influences. Andrew lives on the South Downs with his partner, Sue.

Paul Brownsey lives in Bearsden, Glasgow. He is a former lecturer in Philosophy at Glasgow University. His book, *His Steadfast Love and Other Stories* (Lethe Press, USA) was a Lambda Literary Awards finalist and received a starred review from *Publishers Weekly*. Recent work has appeared in *Event*, *upstreet* and *Ambit*.

Ian Inglis was born in Stoke-on-Trent and now lives in Newcastle upon Tyne. As a Reader in Sociology and Visiting Fellow at Northumbria University, he is the author of several books and many articles around topics within popular culture. His short fiction has appeared in numerous anthologies and literary magazines.

Eileen Jones lives in Tynedale. She had a short play produced by New Writing North in 2006, poetry pamphlet, *Connecting Flight* published by *Red Squirrel Press* and collection, *The Pale Handbag of the Apocalypse,* (IRON 2014). She has co-edited IRON anthologies, including *Cold IRON – Ghost Stories from the Twenty First Century (*2017) and *The IRON Book of Tree Poetry* (2020).

Sarah Tanburn writes short stories, novels, poetry, reviews and essays. Her work has been published widely, including by New Welsh Review, Snapshots of History, Ink Sweat & Tears, River of Stones, Nation Cymru and Ether Books. She is now working on a maritime novel, drawing on her own experience at sea.

Pauline Plummer has lived in the North East since the 1980s. Poetry is her first love. Her verse novella, *From Here to Timbuktu* (Smokestack Books 2012) was a Read Regional choice. Her stories are published in anthologies from Comma Press, New Writing North, The Journal and IRON Press. Her own collection is *Dancing With a Stranger* (Red Squirrel Press 2014).

Rieve Atkinson lives in rural West Cornwall. He's been published in many literary magazines, broadcast on BBC Radio 4, and has read at UK literary festivals. His 2015 collection *Spaces* was published by Gaudy Prawn Press. In 2019, he received the Gorsedh Kernow gold medal for poetry.

Gerry Webber is a member of the Stobie Stories writing group in Edinburgh and has previously been published in Far Off Places and the Anti-Zine. Raised in South London, he now lives in Scotland where he enjoys a life of economic inactivity. Somehow, he is married with two grown up children.

Robert Rayner joined Northumbrian Writers' Group on retirement, after a legal career in local government. He has achieved success in a number of writing competitions. His other interests include following Newcastle United, Parkrun, reading, travel, and rambling. He also enjoys real ale, robust red wines and spending time with his family.

Judith Wall became interested in writing after a varied career in Primary teaching in different parts of the country. She now belongs to various writing groups and develops her ideas from her UK and foreign travel.

Gerald Cole is a freelance journalist and author of 14 books, including filmographies, a novel, a co-written autobiography, a self-build manual and numerous film and TV novelizations, one of which, *Gregory's Girl*, became a GCE set text. A lifelong SF fan, he's delighted to be a contributor to the *Aliens* anthology.

IRON Press is among the country's longest
established independent literary publishers.
The press began operations in 1973 with IRON
Magazine which ran for 83 editions until 1997.
Since 1975 we have also brought out a regular list
of individual collections of poetry, fiction and
drama plus various anthologies including
*Voices of Conscience, Limerick Nation,
The Poetry of Perestroika, 100 Island Poems,
Cold Iron – Ghost Stories from the 21st Century*
and *The IRON Book of Tree Poems.*

The press is one of the leading independent
publishers of haiku in the UK.
Since 2013 we have also run a biennial IRON
Press Festival round the harbour in our
native Cullercoats. The IRON OR Festival took
place in June 2019. We hope to stage festival No.5
to celebrate our 50th Anniversary in 2023.

We are delighted to be a part of Inpress Ltd, which
was set up by Arts Council England to support
independent literary publishers.
Go to our website (www.ironpress.co.uk)
for full details of our titles and activities.